PRAISE FOR
ZEN MEDITATION IN PLAIN ENGLISH

"Here is a lucid guide to the first step of any serious spiritual journey. All of the usual fat that accompanies works of this type has been trimmed away, leaving the bones and marrow—the essentials that any newcomer needs to know to enter the way."
John Daido Loori Roshi
Abbot of Zen Mountain Monastery

"Authentic Zen meditation is easy if you are given clear, step-by-step instructions. This wonderful book gives just such instructions and teaches you how to calm your body, breath, and mind. Follow these steps, and right here, now, you will be on the path of the ancient Zen masters."
Sensei Wendy Egyoku Nakao
Abbot of Zen Center of Los Angeles

"John Buksbazen's book is an authentic presentation of a universal and timeless teaching, particularly valuable because of the practical clarity and warmth of its style."
Dennis Genpo Merzel Roshi
Abbott of Kanzeon Zen Center

"Clear, simple, and well-grounded in years of experience, Daishin's book is a real gift to anyone interested in Zen practice."
Bernie Glassman Roshi,
Founder of the Zen Peacemaker Order

ZEN MEDITATION
IN PLAIN ENGLISH

ZEN MEDITATION IN PLAIN ENGLISH

By John Daishin Buksbazen

Foreword by Peter Matthiessen

WISDOM PUBLICATIONS • BOSTON

Wisdom Publications
199 Elm St.
Somerville, MA 02144 USA
www.wisdompubs.org

Library of Congress Cataloging-in-Publication Data
Buksbazen, John Daishin, 1939–
    Zen meditation in plain English / by John Daishin Buksbazen ;
foreword by Peter Matthiessen.
      p. cm.
    Includes bibliographical references.
    ISBN 0-86171-316-8 (alk. paper)
    1. Meditation—Zen Buddhism. I. Title
BQ9288.B846 2002
294.3'435—dc21   2001055944

ISBN 0-86171-316-8

First Edition
07 06 05 04 03 02
7   6   5   4   3   2

Cover design by Suzanne Heiser
Interior design by Gopa & Ted2
Interior illustrations by Andrew Campbell

To my teachers,
Taizan Maezumi Roshi,
Roshi Bernie Glassman,
Sensei Wendy Egyoku Nakao;

to my wife
Concetta F. Alfano;

and to my dear friend
Rick Fields,

this book is gratefully dedicated.
You showed me the Way.

TABLE OF CONTENTS

ACKNOWLEDGMENTS

S PECIAL THANKS to my editor at Wisdom Publications, Josh Bartok, without whose patient and writer-friendly guidance this book would not have ripened as it did.

Great appreciation also to my Dharma teacher and Abbot of Buddha Essence Temple, the Zen Center of Los Angeles, Sensei Wendy Egyoku Nakao, for her encouragement and support throughout this project and in my life. And to my wife, Concetta, for who she is.

I am also most grateful to the sangha of ZCLA, and especially to my fellow Zen practice instructors, for their help in putting together the Frequently Asked Questions section of this book.

FOREWORD
Peter Matthiessen

THIS GENTLE BOOK, reflecting the wise teachings of Taizan Maezumi Roshi, is a wonderful introduction to Zen Buddhism, and also an invitation to new life. To practice Zen means to realize one's existence in the beauty and clarity of this present moment, rather than letting life unravel in useless daydreaming of the past and future. To "rest in the present" is a state of magical simplicity, although attainment of this state is not as simple as it sounds: most of us need dedicated training under the guidance of a roshi (a Zen master) in order to let the debris of existence fall away. From the very beginning, the sitting meditation called zazen will bring about a strong sense of well-being, as body and mind return to natural harmony with all creation; later there comes true insight into the nature of existence, which is no different from one's own true nature, or the nature of the Buddha—whose name means "The-One-Who-Knows."

Zen has been called "the religion before religion," which is to say that anyone can practice, even those committed to another faith. And the phrase evokes that natural religion of our early childhood, when heaven and a splendorous earth were one. For the new child in the light of spring, there is no self to forget; the eye with which he sees God, in Meister Eckhart's phrase, is the eye with which God sees him. But that clear eye is soon clouded over by ideas and opinions, preconceptions and abstractions, and simple being becomes encrusted with the armor of ego. Not until years later does an instinct come that a vital sense of mystery has been withdrawn. The sun glints through the pines, and the heart is pierced in a moment of beauty and strange pain, like a memory of paradise.

After that day, there is no beauty without pain, and at the bottom of each breath, there is a hollow place that is filled with longing. That day we become seekers without knowing that we seek, and at first, we long for something "greater" than ourselves, something far away. It is not a return to childhood, for childhood is not a truly enlightened state; yet to seek one's own true nature is, as one Zen master has said, "a way to lead you to your long-lost home."

Most of us cast about for years until something in our reading, some stray word, points to the vague outlines of a path. Perhaps this book is the beginning of your homeward way; if so, count yourself lucky, for it offers no tangled analyses, no solutions, only the way to forgetting the self, the way to zazen, to "just sitting." Through zazen, ideas dissolve, the mind becomes transparent, and in the great stillness of samadhi (Melville called it, "that profound silence, that only voice of God"), there comes an intuitive understanding that what we seek lies nowhere else but in this present moment, right here now where we have always been, in the common miracle of our own divinity. To travel this path, one need not be a "Zen Buddhist"—call yourself a zazen Buddhist if you like! "Zen Buddhist" is only another idea to be discarded, like "enlightenment," or "Buddha," or "God."

INTRODUCTION

ZEN BUDDHISM, according to various authorities, is a religion, or a philosophy, or a way of life, or a mental and physical discipline. Some say it is all of the above; others say it is none.

Fundamentally, Zen is a way of seeing clearly who we are and what our life is, and a way of living based on that clear vision.

Many people wonder what Zen is all about, and how it works. They find much of the literature about Zen confusing and are unclear about how it applies to daily living.

This book is in large measure directed to those people. Its aim is to give enough information to get them started in Zen practice, especially in the form of seated meditation called *zazen* or just "sitting." The assumption is that this practice will do more for the inquiring individual than reading any number of books or articles. Once actual practice has begun, then books (carefully chosen for their relevance and reliability) can enrich and broaden one's understanding. But if there is not a sound foundation of experience, then the books will remain undigested in the domain of intellect, and not be of much use.

After all, cookbooks are fun to read, but they aren't very nutritious. They are most helpful to somebody who is actually involved in cooking.

So once you've read this book, the next step is to start practice. If your community has a Zen teacher, so much the better. If not, then you are on your own until you find one, and encouraging you to do that is another of the aims of this book. It is intended to give you enough information to get you started and keep you going until you can find and begin practice with a qualified teacher, either of Zen or of one of the related practices, such as Insight Meditation or Tibetan Buddhism.

Keep this in mind, though: sooner or later, you really must study with a teacher, for the practice is long and not easy, and there are many opportunities to become discouraged or confused along the way.

Also, as you progress you will have experiences you'll want to discuss and questions that should be reliably answered. This process should be addressed on a personal basis by a qualified teacher who knows you and can deal with you directly. But this book can keep you going until you and your teacher meet.

USING THIS BOOK

Beyond reading this book and thinking about it, there is another way to use it.

I've written it as conversationally as possible, so that you can imagine you're at a Zen center receiving the kind of introductory instruction commonly offered to new sitters. One good way to use the book is to get together with a group of your friends who share your interest in beginning to meditate, and to take turns reading the instructions aloud while the entire group actually follows them step by step.

Somehow even though you may have read the words silently to yourself, they make more of an impact if you can also absorb them through the sense of hearing. Go slowly enough so that everyone in the group has plenty of time to follow each step. Pause often, and don't rush. Allow plenty of time to cover the material, and don't hesitate to repeat a section until it is clear to everyone. You'll often find that hearing a passage for the fifth or even the tenth time will give you new information.

If you're alone, you may find it helpful to make a recording of these instructions, so that you can instruct yourself as you go.

This book is divided into three main sections, followed by answers to some frequently asked questions, and some useful appendices. The three main sections are: "Buddhas," "Sitting," and "Community."

The first section deals with the experiences and teaching career of the historical Buddha, Shakyamuni, as well as briefly discussing the unbroken line of teachers who have been his successors through more than eighty generations down to the present day.

The second section focuses on the practice of sitting meditation itself. It sets forth detailed instructions on how to do it and places sitting in the context of an overall practice.

The third section extends those individual practices and discoveries to a larger community, providing the vital link between the individual and the society in which he or she exists.

Hopefully, by carefully reading all three sections, you will begin to get a sense of Zen practice as a whole, and the way it functions in everyday life.

PART ONE:
BUDDHAS

BACKGROUND

THE STORY OF
SHAKYAMUNI BUDDHA

ABOUT TWENTY-FIVE hundred years ago in India, the son of a wealthy and powerful nobleman made a profound discovery. Dissatisfied with his sheltered existence, and deeply troubled by the problems of life and death and the human suffering all around him, he left his family compound and set off upon a journey of self-exploration and study. And after many years of rigorous asceticism and scholarly philosophical research, he still had to admit that he was unable to answer a fundamental question: "What is life-and-death all about?"

At that point, he abandoned his previous practices of fasting, self-mortification, and intellectual inquiry. He decided that the only way for him to really grapple with that question was to grapple directly with himself.

So he stopped fasting, bathed himself, had a bowl of milk (which really shocked his fellow ascetics!), and looked for the answer within. For six years, we are told, his main activity was sitting motionless hour after hour, looking deeply into his own mind. Now he knew he was on the right track; he could feel it as he grew steadier and stronger in his meditation. But even though he was determined, it still took a lot of hard work for him not to become discouraged and not to wander off into some other activity.

But he kept at it steadily and one day sensed that he was reaching a crisis. He simply had to break through whatever it was that separated him from realization of the Truth. And so it was, in that frame of mind, that he sat down under a tree and vowed to not rise until he had either answered his burning question or died in the attempt.

Sitting there, he focused his whole attention upon that question and became so absorbed in his consuming inquiry that he lost track of everything else. He didn't even think of himself or about the nature of the question; he was too busy questioning. He and the question no longer seemed to be two different things. It was as though he had totally become one with the question, had become the questioning itself.

On the morning of December the eighth, as he sat there in deep meditation, he caught a glimpse of the morning star—the planet Venus—alone in the empty sky at dawn. And at that moment, something tremendous happened. He suddenly *was* that morning star, suddenly was the whole universe itself. Of course, this experience could have been precipitated by almost anything else: a chirping bird, a passing dog, a stubbed toe. In fact, almost any phenomenon could have triggered his breakthrough once he had become sufficiently concentrated and focused upon his question. But in the case of the man called Siddhartha Gotama Shakyamuni, the stimulus was seeing the planet Venus. At that point, his question vanished, and he knew. It was as though he had suddenly awakened from a dream and was able to see reality directly for the first time.

And from then on, people called him Buddha, which simply means "The One Who Woke Up."

We must see our life clearly.
The existence of this very moment—
what is it?
Maezumi Roshi

THE LINEAGE

The Buddha spent the rest of his life, nearly fifty years more, telling and showing people how they too could wake up by making the same discovery he had made. Gradually others came to practice sitting in meditation as he had taught it and found for themselves the experience of realizing who they truly were and what life and death were about on the most fundamental level.

Through the years following his breakthrough, many of his followers made the same discovery. But it was not until late in his teaching career that the Buddha was satisfied that one of his disciples had really deepened and clarified his understanding sufficiently to carry on the teaching independently. Once he had found this person, a man named Mahakashyapa, the Buddha publicly named him as the successor to his own understanding, to his own state of mind.

This man, Mahakashyapa, in turn waited until he too could confidently name one of his disciples as successor, able to provide fully reliable instruction and guidance to future students.

And so it went, each successor in turn training many students and always looking for one or more of them who would have a deep and clear enough understanding and the right personal qualities to carry on the teaching.

This went on for twenty-eight generations in India, before one of these successors, Bodhidharma, finally found his way to China, bringing with him the practice of sitting. After six generations in China, the teaching spread to Korea, the rest of Asia, and eventually to Japan. What's most important to keep in mind about this continuation of the teachings is that it was never based upon purely intellectual study or secondhand understanding; always the individuals who were entrusted with the responsibility to transmit Buddhism properly were those whose practice and realization were outstanding, and who had thoroughly grasped the essence of each phase of the teaching. Additionally, the personality of the individual must be especially suited to the task of teaching others. With these conditions satisfied, the person could then become a successor in the teaching lineage of his or her teacher.

It is this unbroken line of teachers and their successors that has helped ensure that the enlightenment of the historical Buddha has continued through more than eighty generations from India through China to Japan and now to the Western world.

It is essential that one practice under the guidance of an authentic representative of this succession if one wishes to attain to a deep and clear understanding of life and death.

No one can live your life except you.
No one can live my life except me.
You are responsible. I am responsible.
But what is our life? What is our death?
Maezumi Roshi

BUDDHAS IN AMERICA

That Zen has been transmitted across culture and continents reminds us that Buddhism is not some alien Oriental mystery that we as Westerners cannot understand. It has come to us from Asia, but the point is that we here in the West can now participate in this practice, not as foreigners dipping into an unfamiliar culture, but in our own right, as ourselves, dipping into ourselves. When this takes place, Buddhism is as natural and indigenous to the West as are those who practice it.

Today, as much as anyone ever before, we are concerned with the kinds of questions the Buddha was asking. We seem to be searching for some basic principle to tie everything together. We want this principle to be something that helps us to live and to grow harmoniously and sanely in an increasingly difficult world.

Being of a practical turn of mind, we don't want to settle for concepts alone, for vague emotional generalities, or to accept secondhand the insights of somebody else, no matter how revered or respected that other person might be. We want to find out for ourselves, directly, clearly, and without doubt, just who we are, what our life is, and exactly what difference that clarity makes.

In the day-to-day, month-to-month, year-to-year practice with a teacher who embodies that realization we find the inspiration and guidance that the students of Buddhism have always sought from and found in their teachers. And after the kind of training and realization that repeated contact with a teacher offers, the student ultimately is able to take enlightenment itself as teacher and guide, having discovered who he or she really is, having forgotten the narrow self.

Shakyamuni Buddha urged his students not to depend upon others, but to look to themselves for liberation. Seventeen centuries later, the great Japanese Zen master Dogen taught:

To study the Buddha way is to study the self.
To study the self is to forget the self.
To forget the self is to be enlightened by the myriad things.

Here, in these pages, is how to get started doing just that.

Zazen is the practice and realization
of manifesting our body as bodhi, as enlightenment.
It is both the practice and the realization, for when we truly do zazen,
there is no distinction between practice and realization. It is wisdom
as is, as things are. This zazen, the practice of the Buddha Way,
is none other than the practice of one's life.
Maezumi Roshi

PART TWO:
SITTING

THE PROBLEM
AND ITS SOLUTION

THE NATURE OF THE PROBLEM

WHEN SHAKYAMUNI BUDDHA first experienced enlightenment, he exclaimed that it was amazing, miraculous, and wonderful that all beings had the same wisdom and compassion as the fully awakened one, but that since their perceptions were distorted they could not see this directly.

What he meant was that we tend to create a problem for ourselves by our accustomed way of thinking, and by the ingrained bias of our perceptions, but beneath all that we are perfect.

When we compulsively split ourselves and the world into prefabricated categories such as "good" and "bad," "us" and "them," "real" and "ideal," we discover we have gotten into serious difficulties.

It isn't so terrible to think logically and to be analytical; if we are designing a bridge or balancing a checkbook, that's the best way to think and the best way to be. But when we look carefully, we see that discursive, linear thinking is only useful for certain kinds of tasks; for others it is quite useless. Like the hammer or the toothbrush, discursive thought is a tool intended for certain kinds of jobs: If you use a hammer to brush your teeth, or a toothbrush to drive nails, you are not likely to meet with great success.

The problem for most of us born into this culture is that we are very strongly conditioned and taught, from infancy onward, to rely almost totally upon discursive logic and rational thought. We are sometimes even discouraged from developing or relying on our innate ability to grasp reality intuitively and directly. Such abilities may be labeled "unscientific" by many, and dismissed as incomprehensible mysticism or mere imagination. Even when trying to deal with questions of ultimate values and purposes, when trying to approach ultimate reality, we are often urged to remain in the modes of thought learned early in our social education and not to entrust ourselves to other ways of knowing reality.

So it is that we are taught to disown and lose contact with an extremely important aspect of ourselves, our intuitive and direct knowledge, and to rely entirely and to our own detriment on only one aspect, our intellect. As a result, we are forever separating from ourselves, stepping back a few paces and looking at rather than simply being, who we are.

And as we do that, we create a split, a gap that we experience as alienation, or loneliness, or boredom, or frustration, or craving, or revulsion. We look into a mirror and see individual "selves" encased in skin-prisons and doomed perpetually to solitary confinement. Of course, we have such a wonderful assortment of entertainments and pastimes in our prisons that we manage to divert ourselves from that wan awareness much of the time. But sooner or later in most lives, there comes a time when the individual senses, more or less painfully, that something is fundamentally not quite right. Our tendency is then to look for and define the sources of the problem in social, political, economic, or interpersonal terms. Even when in traditional Western psychology we "turn inward," we generally choose to deal with our memories and feelings in terms of interactions with others, seeing ourselves as acted-upon and our experiences as at least partially determined by forces outside our control.

Because there is some truth here, we tend to cling to these ideas, subtly organizing our lives around them, unconsciously married to them and depending upon them as if for our very lives. Many of us never go further than this. But a growing number of us are finding this approach to understanding life ultimately unsatisfying, inadequate in dealing with life's truly fundamental questions. Sometimes we may feel that our life consists of too many events, all passing so rapidly that it's difficult to keep track of them all. The world around us keeps changing, from moment to moment; people come and go, circumstances shift constantly—how can we respond appropriately to all of it?

The world around us is actually no more complex or busy than our own internal world filled as it is with sensations, impulses, thoughts, memories, fantasies, wishes, hopes, fears. Within us, all these experiences arise and change from one moment to the next in a dizzying dance with the events of the outer world. Rarely are we aware of the ways this dance affects our interactions with the world around us or the world within.

We become so familiar with this whirlwind of events that we imagine it simply is "the way things are," never pausing to question our ceaseless reactivity. And yet as time goes on, we find ourselves becoming more and more fatigued by commonplace occurrences, and increasingly stressed out by daily events. At times our lives may seem like nothing more than an endless round of conditioned actions and reactions; at other times, we may simply turn away from this disheartening view and try to lose ourselves in the surface of our lives.

And yet, after years of this, we may feel an inkling that we have overlooked something in the midst of so much busyness. Perhaps we don't quite know exactly what is missing, but we know we miss it.

At times it may seem that if only we could call a "time out" from the continual demands on our attention and energies, if we could somehow just take a break from constantly having to deal with one thing after another, then perhaps we might get a glimpse of what we were looking for. And so we may attempt to shift gears: a change of scene, a vacation, a new hobby, some alteration in our usual routines. We make some outward change in the hope it will bring us closer to some peace with the outer world, equilibrium within, or a vantage point from which we will be able to make more sense of our lives, to see ourselves more clearly. But inevitably the vacation ends, the novelty becomes familiar, and the change, routine. Thus the merry-go-round begins again.

And so eventually we begin to look for a more radical approach, a response that penetrates to the very roots of our existence, rather than merely remaining focused on the branches and leaves.

In studying ourselves,
we find the harmony
that is our total existence.
We do not make harmony.
We do not achieve it or gain it.
It is there all the time.
Here we are, in the midst of this perfect way,
and our practice is simply to realize it and then
to actualize it
in our everyday life.
Maezumi Roshi

THE NATURE OF THE SOLUTION

Sitting is just such a radical approach, a way of getting deeply in touch with the true Self. Not just with the narrow self; that much can be accomplished through psychotherapy or a number of other disciplines. But sitting deals with the "big-S"–Self, that most basic level of reality that has nothing to do with culture, social status, intellect, or even personality. It deals with who you really are beyond all the specifics of time and place. And who you really are, ultimately, is the universe itself.

But sitting is also much more than a method of experiencing the Self in this way. Sitting itself is also a direct expression of what it was that Shakyamuni Buddha found out—of what it is that you, yourself a buddha, find out. That's why you'll discover that sitting is not only a tool, a means toward an end, but that it is also a way of life that is a living model of living itself.

*The best way to practice
is to forget the self.*
Maezumi Roshi

THE PRACTICE

STARTING TO SIT

WHEN YOU BEGIN to sit, it is best not to try to do too much right away. If you begin by sitting about fifteen (or even ten!) minutes a day, that's enough. You'll be less likely to wear yourself out or get discouraged that way. Build up your sitting time very gradually, perhaps a minute longer every few days, until you can sit reasonably well for about a half-hour at a time.

And remember, it's not nearly as important how long you sit as it is how regularly and vigorously you sit, and how carefully you follow the instructions in this book on the practice of zazen.

It's much better to "sit hard" every day for a half-hour or so than to sit for an hour or two several times a month.

"Sitting hard" simply means that even when you don't feel particularly enthusiastic or in the mood for sitting, you still sit down and do your level best. Even if you have a rough time of it, you can be assured that that kind of sincere effort will be quite effective.

In fact, you are likely to find out gradually that not only are all the "problems" you encounter in trying to sit well quite natural, but that the process of encountering those "problems" is, in itself, the life of your sitting practice. I put the word "problems" in quotation marks, because difficulties only become problems when we separate ourselves from them instead of dealing with them directly and wholeheartedly.

The difference between "problems" and mere difficulties rests in relating to your situation openly and skillfully. Letting yourself simply experience your difficulties without getting caught up in thoughts about how much you dislike them and in wishes that you didn't have to deal with them in the first place will change your experience of difficulties. But be very clear about this: It's not a matter of denying discomfort or resisting unfavorable circumstances; it is simply being willing to relate to all things just as they are—and practicing anyway. Even if your sitting doesn't always come easily—as it surely won't!—just view everything as a helpful lesson, take all experience as it comes, without comment, neither clinging to it nor running away. This is the nature of the practice of sitting.

The moment-to-moment fluctuations in our concentration, comfort, and enthusiasm are natural, simply reflecting the reality of our experience at any given point. And essentially there's nothing wrong with that, as long as we refrain from editorializing and criticizing. Our task is to accept each moment and move on from there, continuing to do our level best. When sitting is difficult, the thing to avoid is buying into our inevitable feelings of frustration or discouragement. And when sitting seems to be going well, we just accept that too in an equally matter-of-fact way, without becoming euphoric. We must let go of all ideas of "making progress" or "not making progress." Easy or hard, take each moment as it is, accepting it as a helpful teaching, without comment. This is the heart of learning to sit, and this is the way we learn to appreciate our life.

In zazen we do not expect anything.
Zazen is not a technique to achieve anything.
It is much more natural. And yet, somehow the most natural thing
is difficult to do. How come? Because we think.
There is nothing wrong with thinking.
Thinking is a very natural process,
but we are so easily conditioned
by our thinking and give
too much value to it.
Maezumi Roshi

LAYING THE FOUNDATIONS

When you begin to sit, you need to be quite careful about how you arrange your legs, how your spine is adjusted, where you place your hands, and other seemingly unimportant details. It's like laying the foundation for a building—if the foundation is not level and properly lined up, the whole structure will be shaky. So even if you have a little trouble getting the position right, be patient and careful with yourself, so that you can get settled into a good posture for sitting.

Appendix I offers several suggestions of exercises to help you limber up. But, as in whatever you do, don't go to extremes. Sitting isn't meant to be a form of self-abuse or torture! Nor is it meant to be practiced casually at irregular intervals. Just work at it daily for a moderate length of time, and let your practice grow at a natural pace.

SOME RULES OF THUMB

More will be said about these in what follows, but here are some rules of thumb for sitting:

1. When you sit, try to make your body into a tripod or pyramid shape by making a three-pointed base of your two knees and your buttocks. Unless you sit in a chair (which is discussed later), both knees should stay in contact with the floor at all times when sitting.

2. Once you've gotten seated, your spine should be erect, not stiffly as in a military brace position, but not slumped over into an exaggerated S-curve either.

3. Your torso should be perpendicular to the floor, not leaning to the right or left, or forward or backward. The same thing applies to your head; it should rest squarely atop your spine, and not tilt in any direction.

4. Wear loose, baggy clothes when sitting, so you don't cut off your circulation or constrict the breathing movement of your rib cage or the muscles of your lower belly.

SITTING SUPPORTS

One last note, before you get started: In sitting, two items of equipment are recommended: a pill-shaped cushion called a *zafu*, or
alternatively a wooden kneeling support, called a *seiza* bench, and
a thick rectangular mat called a *zabuton*. The seiza bench is often
more comfortable for a "kneeling-while-sitting-on-the-heels" position, since it takes the weight of the body off the ankles completely,
and provides a firm support. But while very helpful, even this
equipment isn't strictly necessary; you can fold up a couple of old
blankets to make a reasonable substitute for these items. The only
thing to keep in mind about cushions is that you should avoid
foam rubber or other synthetics because they tend to lack the firm-
ness of kapok or buckwheat hulls (the usual fillings for zafus) and
will give you a wobbly seat.

When you sit, your zafu (or seiza bench) goes on top of the zabuton, and you sit on the zafu or bench. But don't sit squarely in the
middle of the zafu; rather use it as a kind of wedge under your buttocks, using only the forward third of the zafu to actually support
you. This will help you place the weight of your body more toward
a central area between the three points of your tripod-base, and
relieve some strain on your spinal column.

POSITIONING THE BODY

Now let's look at the various positions in which you can sit. Try them
all out, and pick the one that works best for you at your present

stage of development and flexibility. Don't try to force your legs into the full- or half-lotus if they really just won't go.

There's no value in hurting yourself. Zazen, in fact, should be comfortable.

We will examine each position in detail shortly. In order of difficulty, the sitting positions are:

• the full-lotus position
(this one's the toughest but the most stable);

• the half-lotus position
(almost as stable, and a little easier);

• the Burmese position
(not quite as stable, as we'll see, but much easier);

• seiza or kneeling position
(quite easy for most folks);

• sitting in a chair
(especially recommended for sitters who, because of age, illness, or physical condition, cannot sit in any of the above positions.)

POSITIONING THE LEGS

In setting out directions for sitting in these positions, we'll first describe in some detail the arrangement of the legs. Once your legs are arranged in the position you've decided to use, the rest of the instructions pretty much apply equally to all the positions.

The Full-Lotus Position

The full-lotus position is the best way to sit for a number of reasons. It's the best position in terms of supporting the spine most firmly and thus helping one sit in an upright enough posture for extended periods of meditation with minimal additional effort. Since the pelvis is automatically tucked under in this position, the sitter generally finds it less necessary to make corrections to the spine's position during a period of sitting, so the lotus position also helps in concentration. The difficulty for many, however, is that we are generally unused to the position of the legs, and find it literally a bit of a stretch, which can make it, at least initially, uncomfortable or even painful. For those who wish to, stretching and yoga exercises can gradually enable the body to adjust to this posture.

In the long run, it is also the most comfortable of all the positions, once you get used to sitting that way. And of course, that's the main difficulty. Getting into this position and getting used to it are often too tough for new sitters, who find their legs hurt so badly that they just can't make this position at all. This is mostly due to the tightness of your leg muscles. With steady practice, you'll loosen up considerably.

If at first you can't get into the full-lotus position, don't push yourself, for there is a real chance of hurting yourself if you go too far too fast. A general rule is: Do it if you feel only mild discomfort, but don't do it if you feel severe pain.

Once you've seated yourself upon the zafu, place your right foot on your left thigh, and the left foot on the right (or vice-versa if more comfortable). Make sure your heels are drawn up as close to your abdomen as possible, rather than letting your feet slip down toward the inside of the thighs or the calves. In this position, the soles of both your feet should tend to point at the ceiling. If at all possible, the toes of both feet should project freely beyond the thigh, so that they can be wiggled without encountering any resistance.

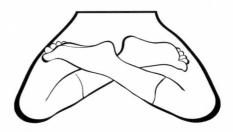

The legs crossed
in the full-lotus position.
This is the most difficult position to get into,
but the most stable to maintain.
Remember: Never force your body
into a position it doesn't want to take.

The Half-Lotus Position

This position is basically the same as the full-lotus, except that the right foot is tucked under the left thigh and rests upon the floor (or the zabuton if you're using one), while the left foot goes on top of the right thigh or the right calf. This position is usually easier than the full-lotus to get into when you're first starting out, since less pressure is put on the knees and legs. The disadvantage, however, is that this position isn't as balanced as the full-lotus, since one foot is up on the thigh and the other is under the thigh on the ground. The result is a tendency for your body to tilt slightly to one side, which must be compensated for very carefully when you get into the position. This compensation happens when you reach the stage of swaying to find your center (see page 50). Also, one knee will tend to rise into the air, and you'll have to use a higher zafu so that both knees rest solidly upon the floor or zabuton. Generally speaking, the further you go from the full-lotus, the higher your zafu should be. (Naturally, this doesn't apply to sitting in a chair or in the kneeling position.)

Finally, since your pelvis isn't as well supported in this position, it'll be easier for your back to slump and curve, thus spoiling your posture. But if you're aware of these difficulties and make the necessary adjustments, you'll find the half-lotus to be a very effective sitting position, and one that will help you get ready for the full-lotus as time goes by. In order to make this position even more of a help, try reversing your legs every other time you sit; that is, instead of having the left foot up and the right foot under, put the right foot up and the left under. That will increase flexibility in both legs and be a big help to your sitting.

The Burmese Position

In the Burmese position, draw the right foot up close to the left thigh (or vice-versa), allowing the foot and calf to rest on the floor or zabuton. Then place the left foot in front of the right calf so that both knees touch the mat. If your knees don't reach the mat, try using a higher zafu, and if this doesn't help, you might consider placing support cushions under your knees.

Usually, this position is much easier to get into than either the full- or half-lotus positions. It certainly is much easier on the legs.

But because it really doesn't do much to support your pelvis and spine in the proper alignment, it tends to be most tiring to the back over a long period of time. Nonetheless, it's a good position for beginners, and even experienced sitters find that they can do good sitting in the Burmese position.

In order to make this position work, you just have to be more careful with your back, and be alert for the first signs that your posture is beginning to slump so that you can correct it.

Also remember that this position requires the highest zafu of all the positions. Some folks just put one zafu on top of another, and that's okay to do. But pay attention to your back! If if doesn't hurt when you sit for a half-hour, fine. But if you get any pain or stiffness there, then you need to correct your posture.

The legs bent
in the Burmese position.
You may find it more comfortable
with the positions of the left and right legs reversed.

The Seiza or Kneeling Position

Traditional seiza position is done without external support, and the weight of the body is distributed between the knees and heels. Most

Westerners find this position difficult to maintain for extended periods of time, and so we have incorporated the use of either a zafu or a special seiza bench for sitting in this position, which makes it quite comfortable for many of us.

To sit seiza with a zafu, kneel with the zafu *sideways on its edge* between your heels (see below). Then sit back, as though to sit on your heels, and let the zafu bear the weight of your body. Using a seiza bench is similar, except that the bench is placed over the calves while kneeling, thus suspending the greatest part of body mass between the heels and the knees, and sparing the ankles from having to support your weight. Many find the seiza bench a great help in maintaining this position, since it takes up the weight of the body while providing a very stable seat.

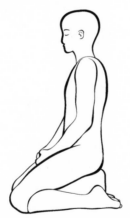

Kneeling in the seiza position.
Most people can easily assume the position,
either on a seiza bench
or a zafu on its side.

Remember that the basic model is the tripod or pyramid, so keep your knees far enough apart to give you a steady base. Otherwise this posture will be hard to maintain and you'll wobble around, which is not helpful to your sitting or concentration.

Often it helps, especially if you're sitting more than one period, to alternate positions from one period to the next. That way you spread the stress more evenly, and your legs won't get quite as tired as they might if you sit in only one position.

Sitting in a Chair

People often seem to feel reluctant about sitting in a chair, as though it were less authentic or spiritual to do it that way than with legs crossed on the floor.

Actually, even though chair-sitting has its own problems, there is no reason why you can't sit quite well in a chair, either temporarily until you get in shape for floor-sitting, or as your sole zazen position if your age, physique, or condition require it.

As in other positions, the important thing is to get yourself perpendicular to the floor and to straighten the spine.

The tough part about chair-sitting is that it's very easy to slump, then slouch, and finally collapse against the chair-back. And that's not good.

The best kind of chair to use is a plain, unupholstered, wooden kitchen chair, a simple piano bench or a stool without a back. Just place your zafu on the seat of the chair or bench.

Sit on the forward third of the seat, so that your back is not touching the back of the chair and your knees are slightly lower

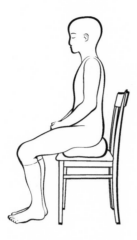

Sitting in a chair.
It's actually easier to maintain this position
if you don't lean back in your chair.

than your hips. Having your hips higher than your knees is actually quite important, since it allows your lower belly to expand and contract freely, thus encouraging unconstricted breathing. Next, place your feet squarely on the floor, about the same distance apart as your shoulders. Let your hands rest comfortably upon your thighs near the belly.

A special elevated meditation bench is also made, similar to a seiza bench but the height of chair, slanted to properly align the hips.

POSITIONING THE REST OF THE BODY

By now you've learned about how the legs are arranged in all of the five sitting positions. From here on, instructions for positioning your body are the same no matter how you are sitting.

When you sit, please remind yourself how you can sit best.
When you do that, all the buddhas and ancestors guarantee it is the
right way. Have good trust in yourself,
not in the one that you think you should be,
but in the One that you are.
Maezumi Roshi

Spine

Once you have taken a position and arranged your legs, the next step is to center your spine.

Imagine that your spine is an inverted pendulum, similar to a metronome, hinged at the tailbone, and with your head at the top end as the weight. Swaying in large arcs, move your torso and abdomen first to the left, then right, then left, and so on, as though you were a metronome. Don't let your head move independently, but just make it an extension of your spine, so the air passage from head to body is always aligned and clear from obstruction. And when swaying, always keep your knees firmly planted on the floor or zabuton (except, of course, when sitting in a chair).

Start in a wide arc, and feel the pull of gravity as you reach the outside point of that arc. Sway slowly enough to feel that tug—no use hurrying, so take your time. Can you notice how it seems to decrease as you straighten back up? And when you're in an upright position (perpendicular to the floor), notice that there's practically no sense of pull. Then as you sway over to the other side, notice that pulling sensation return.

Now let the size of the arcs naturally decrease as your momentum dies down, until you just drift to a stop. If you can keep from controlling the rate of speed and the duration of the swings, you will have become a natural plumb line, and will come to rest in a position that is perpendicular to the floor. This will center you properly so that you don't lean in any direction, but are sitting straight. Of course, if you try to speed up or slow down deliberately, what you're actually doing is fighting the laws of gravity and momentum, and you're more likely to wind up sitting crooked, leaning to the side, or straining your back muscles to remain aligned. As always, if you can just harmonize with the laws of nature, you avoid creating such problems.

The next step is to straighten your back. Now normally the spine has a certain degree of curvature to it, and this isn't a problem in itself. You shouldn't try to make your spine ramrod-straight like an iron bar or a yardstick. Not only is that contrary to how human beings are built, but it would tend to cause back trouble over time.

Your main concern now is to let your spine be in the best natural position possible. In that position, your vertebrae aren't all compressed and squashed down upon one another, and you aren't pinching nerves or assuming the posture of exaggerated spinal curvature called lordosis. Here's how to get your back straightened properly.

Imagine that the ceiling is resting on the crown of your head at a point directly over your spine. Now imagine that you are going to act as a tire jack, and that your spine is going to push the ceiling up a little bit. But the action is all in your spine, so be careful not to tense your shoulders or move your head. Just let your spine begin to extend itself, from the base of the spine upward toward the head, carrying the head with it as it straightens. Feel the thrust move upward from the tailbone, and notice that as you do so, there's a tendency to stick your belly out and to let your buttocks protrude backward a bit, as if you were doing a kind of dance.

Now let the energy flow upward, and as you do so, lift that ceiling a half-inch. Don't tilt your head backward or forward, though. Let your spine do the lifting. Push harder. Harder still. Harder. And now relax your effort.

Notice that you stayed erect, that when you relaxed there was no cave-in? That's because you first seated yourself carefully and then centered your spine before you tried to straighten up. If you did all those things quite carefully, according to the instructions, you found that it wasn't necessary after all to use a lot of muscular effort to sit upright and to stay there. Sitting straight and tall and erect is mostly a matter of getting arranged properly, rather than a tug-of-war against gravity.

It's like balancing a bamboo pole on its end; if the pole is perpendicular to the ground, it will remain upright as long as nothing else acts to pull it over. But if the pole is even slightly crooked or out of plumb, it will tend to fall over in that direction unless you reach out and grab it to keep it from falling.

Our bodies are subject to the same law of gravity as that pole. Keeping upright only requires effort if you're using your back muscles to keep yourself erect by brute force, that is, if you are constantly "reaching out and grabbing" yourself to keep from toppling over like a felled pine, slowly and majestically. Your back muscles function like retro-rockets on a spacecraft; they are designed to work for only short periods of time, and in short bursts of effort to make minor course corrections. That's all they can really do. If we demand of our back muscles that they keep us upright steadily for a long time, such as ten or twenty minutes or longer, we are asking too much. Of course, the muscles will obediently try to oblige but will get so fatigued after just a short time that a backache will occur. If you don't heed that warning signal, then muscle spasms and more severe back trouble may result.

In general, back pain is a signal that you aren't sitting quite straight. If you correct your position (by doing the ceiling-pushing-up exercise) you'll generally find the back pain lessening. Always pay attention to back pain or discomfort when sitting and make the necessary postural corrections. Unlike leg discomfort, back pain is significant and should be heeded.

Remember, all these techniques are primarily intended to help you find and keep a comfortable, balanced posture.

The experience of this body and mind as is,
is the plain, universal fact that all the ancient masters realized.
It is the realization that the Way is complete.
Everything is here.
No artificial devices are needed.
Maezumi Roshi

Head and Hands

Having arranged your legs in one of the basic positions, and having centered and straightened your back, the next step is to arrange your head and hands.

This is not very difficult. Since your head is already attached to the end of your spine, you simply allow it to remain there without interference! This means that your head, positioned in line with your spine, should not lean either forward or backward, or to either side. Your ears should be parallel with your shoulders, and the tip of your nose centered over your navel. Tuck your chin in just a little bit, and close your mouth. Now place the tip of your tongue against the roof of your mouth, just behind the front teeth. Swallow your saliva, and evacuate some of the air from your mouth, so that there is a slight vacuum. This will slow down your salivation rate so you won't have to keep swallowing saliva as often as you normally would.

Your eyes should be lowered to approximately a 45-degree angle, neither wide open nor completely closed, but just half-opened and gazing in the direction of the floor about three or four feet ahead of you. (If you're facing the wall and it's closer than three or four feet from you, pretend to be looking through the wall at where the floor would be.) With the eyes in this position, you won't have to blink very often, and you will find that fewer things distract you visually. Generally you're better off not closing your eyes completely, because that tends to make you feel drowsy.

Finally, your hands should be arranged in a special hand position called a mudra. The most common one is called the *cosmic mudra* and is formed as follows.

Place your right hand, palm up, so that the blade of the hand (the part you would strike with in a karate chop) rests against your lower belly. Then place the left hand, palm upward also, on top of the right, so that the middle knuckles overlap and the thumb-tips lightly touch, forming a nice oval frame. (The mudra requires the left hand to be uppermost, since we are subordinating the active principle of the right to the receptive principle of the left. In iconography, conversely, buddhas and bodhisattvas are shown with the right uppermost, indicating their liberating activity.)

The hands positioned
in the cosmic mudra.
You can see the state of your mind
reflected in how you hold your hands.

The positioning of the thumb-tips is important. If your attention wanders, you'll find that the thumbs move apart; and if your sitting has become dull and drowsy, you'll usually find that the thumbs sag in the middle, revealing the loss of alertness. So the thumbs (and your entire posture!) can serve you well as a built-in biofeedback device, continuously reflecting the state of your mind.

Another point to address is the placement of the hands relative to the rest of the body. If you are sitting in the full-lotus position, the heels form a natural base to support the backs of your hands, so that's no problem. But if you are sitting in one of the other positions, you may find that your hands are not symmetrically arranged or that your arms and shoulders get sore from the strain of supporting the hands (which are a little bit on the heavy side) for a full period of sitting. So rather than straining to place your hands in some idealized position, simply let them rest naturally in your lap, as close to the ideal position shown in these drawings as you can get. You can also use a small cushion to rest your mudra on for support. But don't let your hand position be a distraction to you.

ZAZEN CHECKLIST

When your body is in position for sitting, run down this checklist to make sure everything is arranged properly (at first, it may even help to sit in front of a mirror so you can visually check your posture):

1. Sit on the forward third of your zafu.
2. Arrange your legs in the position you can do best.
3. Sway in decreasing arcs to center your spine.
4. Straighten your spine and align your head by doing the ceiling-pushing-up exercise.
5. Lower your eyes and allow them to go out of focus.
6. Close your mouth and position your tongue.
7. Place your hands in the cosmic mudra.
8. Make sure your whole body is arranged properly and comfortably before you begin zazen.

Always remember this rule of thumb: Except for the normal discomfort always associated with a new kind of physical activity, zazen should be comfortable, not agonizing! All of these instructions are intended primarily to help you get and stay comfortable in your sitting. Don't get involved in a competition with yourself (or anyone else) just to see how much pain or how difficult a posture you can take. Be strong and be calm, and pay close attention to what you are doing. Little else is as important as the attitude you bring to sitting.

The complete zazen posture.
Full-lotus position is shown here,
but you should sit in whichever position
is most comfortable for you.

BREATHING

All life depends on breathing, and yet few people really know how to breathe. We are so used to surviving with our regular breathing habits, that we mistake this familiarity of breathing with being able to truly do it well. But what passes for breathing in most of us is more often a kind of panting or gasping.

You've probably noticed that when you run up a couple of flights of stairs or chase a bus, you breathe very heavily, with your chest heaving up and down as you attempt to get enough oxygen. This is obvious panting, and nobody is surprised by it. But when you are sitting still, not straining every muscle for some heavy physical task, there is no real need to continue breathing as though you were running up stairs.

If you are like most people in your breathing habits, you probably breathe about fifteen to eighteen breath-cycles per minute when at rest. This is called your basic breathing rate. It is so common a breathing rate that it is easy to get used to it and to regard it as natural, as though it were the result of how you were constructed in the first place.

But this isn't so.

If you don't fight yourself with poor posture, cramped muscles, squashed internal organs, and an overactive forebrain, you'll find that your breathing will change. It will slow down and become smooth and rhythmic until you are breathing at perhaps five or fewer breath-cycles per minute. And it will do so more effectively if you do not strain or struggle to control your breath.

You don't really need to breathe any more than that when sitting; you're just used to panting because you've had to do that all your life because of improper posture. But when you start sitting regularly, you will naturally connect with the breathing process that maintains your life.

Needless to say, in the profound stillness of zazen, the constant struggle for oxygen is a loud and disturbing whirlwind of activity that keeps us away from genuine stillness. We may discover we have some subtle anxiety at the prospect of stillness, and that rapid breathing or a quickly beating heart are somehow a response to this. But if we let these experiences keep us from sitting, we end up avoiding ourselves without even being aware of trying to do so. The truth is that when we try to avoid ourselves, it is our own life we miss out on.

All day long, we are living the life of the Buddha.
Maezumi Roshi

BREATHING IN ZAZEN

Once you have allowed your body to sit, you must allow your breath to sit as well. Having reached a centered and balanced position, with legs and hands arranged correctly, and with your spine erect, take a few deep breaths and then release them, inhaling through the mouth and exhaling through the nose. These first few breaths will clear your lungs and oxygenate your blood, and will give you a fresh supply of air with which to start. With good posture, you'll find yourself settling into a natural rhythm of breathing, and gradually your breathing will naturally tend to come from the lower abdomen.

Forget about trying to control the flow of air in and out of your body, and just concentrate on being aware of what your breath is doing. Is it fast? That's okay. Is it slow? That's fine. Deep? Great. Shallow? No problem. Just watch what's happening with your breathing and don't try to make corrections. Keep breathing through your nose the way your body tells you to, and let yourself be very clearly aware of all the sensations that accompany the flow of breath in and out of your body.

When you've done this for a few minutes, you'll notice that your upper body and trunk are relaxed and that your breathing has begun to assert its own natural speed and rhythm. In simply allowing this to happen, you'll find that you have begun to breathe much more comfortably. This kind of breathing may well be enough to get you started in your sitting. On the other hand, you may wish at some point to try doing "belly breathing," a type of breathing that especially emphasizes using the abdominal muscles and that can be quite powerful in deepening your concentration. (Either breathing style is quite fine; try both, and see which one works best for you.)

Belly Breathing

Begin sitting as with the natural breathing style, starting with a few deep exhalations and inhalations. When you feel ready to begin belly breathing, here's how:

Focusing your attention in the area of the lower belly, imagine that there's a balloon down there, and that each time you inhale, you're inflating that balloon. Then, as you exhale, imagine that balloon being deflated. Forget about your lungs, chest, and upper torso. They'll take care of themselves. Just concentrate on inflating and deflating that balloon, but at the same time, don't be too force-ful about it. You're not trying to burst the balloon, just inflate it a little!

Feel the air move into that balloon, and feel the walls of the bal-loon bulge outward as the balloon is slowly and steadily inflated. Now let the balloon start to contract inward, as the air moves out of it and through your air passages to be exhaled from the nose. Can you feel movement of the abdominal wall? Keep it steady now. If you're having trouble getting the feel of your lower belly muscles, see page 117, and do the exercise called "abdominal breathing." Then go back to sitting while the memory of how that felt is still fresh in your mind.

Proper breathing involves two basic types of muscular move-ment: horizontal and vertical. The diaphragm moves vertically, and the wall of the lower belly moves horizontally.

The diaphragm is a thick, muscular membrane stretched across the body a little above the midsection. As the diaphragm moves up and down, it alternately pulls air into and pushes air out of the lungs.

At the same time that the diaphragm is moving vertically, the wall of the lower belly swells out slightly. Then as exhalation takes place, the belly wall moves back and actually sinks into the abdomen as the diaphragm moves back up.

To really practice this kind of natural breathing, remember to avoid tight clothing, especially at the waist or chest, so that your breathing movements are not constricted. And also try to avoid eating just before you sit. If your stomach is full of food, it may get in the way of your diaphragm and thus interfere with your breathing.

Actually, that's all there is to it—relaxed yet watchful breathing through the nose and letting the lower belly wall expand with each inhalation and contract with each exhalation. That's all there is to breathing and yet so much is contained within that seemingly simple process.

Imagine that you are making a graph of your breathing. Your "normal" (i.e., habitual) breathing might look like a stock-market graph, with jagged straight lines connecting peaks and valleys, and with steep slopes to show the linear in/out, on/off patterns we've gotten used to over the years.

Now imagine a graph of someone sitting in zazen. The frequency of breathing is reduced, until it goes from approximately fifteen breath-cycles per minute to around four or five breath-cycles per minute.

Note also that the transition from exhaling to inhaling and back again is less definite in zazen breathing than in common "normal" breathing patterns. On our imaginary graph, the lines change from sharp peaks and valleys with steep slopes, to gentle curves.

That's what it means to "regulate" the breath. You simply get out of your own way and allow your body to function naturally without any extra effort. You don't have to be "in control." Marvelously equipped as we are, the process takes care of itself. All you have to do is sit in the proper position and then relax. Gradually you will come to recognize that you yourself *are* the very process of breathing, and nothing extra in the way of gimmicks or techniques is necessary.

Having laid the groundwork of proper body positioning and proper breathing, you are ready to attend to the third aspect of zazen practice: the mind.

THE MIND IN ZAZEN

In some ways, the mind is very much like a pond or a lake. When the water is still and nothing is stirring, the surface of the water becomes smooth as glass and clearly reflects the moon overhead in sharp detail.

But if the water is stirred up, then, for as long as it is stirred up, waves and ripples distort the reflecting surface, until only glimmers of shattered light can be seen. Not until the disturbance dies down can you once again clearly see the reflection of the moon, and thus reality, in its fullness and without distortion.

When you breathe in, swallow the whole universe.
When you breathe out, breathe out the whole universe.
In and out.
In and out.
Eventually you forget about the division between
breathing in and breathing out;
even breathing is totally forgotten.
You just sit with a sense of unity.
Maezumi Roshi

When we sit properly, we still some of the biggest, most obvious waves—those brought about by physical movement. That's why it's important to sit completely still and not fidget. If the body is motionless, it won't create a heavy flow of physical sensations that stir up big waves. Even though we may have some discomfort, or itches, or runny noses, it is worthwhile to relate openly to these in sitting, and not shift, or scratch, or sniffle as we otherwise might. To relate openly means to take each experience as just itself, neither clinging to our opinions or feelings about it, nor trying to avoid it. Various discomforts and dissatisfactions are as much a part of our lives as are our favorite pleasures and satisfactions, and to the extent that we feel compelled to avoid the one and pursue the other, we are not yet living freely. Thus, in zazen we sit as still as we can, maintaining stillness even in the eyes, regardless of the sensations that arise. We are simply aware of and accepting of what comes up, just as it is—without running away from it or clinging to it. This is what sitting is.

That said, it is also important that we not turn our difficulties into occasions for self-abuse. Sitting meditation should not be a contest, with points awarded for technical skill or difficulty; each moment, just sit as yourself, without comparison to some real or imagined ideal other.

Going a step beyond the degree of stillness brought about by an unmoving posture, when you learn to breathe well, you calm the surface of the pond still more and bring yourself that much closer to the mirrorlike state of still water.

But you are still far from mirrorlike reflection as long as your mind is stirred up by fantasies and daydreams, discursive thinking, and all the many forms of ungoverned, uninvited mental activity that seem to go on endlessly in most of us most of the time.

Most of the time, we carry a heavy burden: the thick screen of self-consciousness, continual and acute awareness of our "self" which tends to obscure direct awareness of experiences as they arise and to substitute a focus on oneself as the experiencer, through which everything is filtered. Most of the time, this self-consciousness is so familiar that we don't even notice it. But every once in a while, especially when you first begin to sit, you may find yourself suddenly very much aware of it. Much of what goes on is a matter of continuously evaluating and commenting on whatever happens to capture your attention. It can really get noticeable if you haven't been practicing zazen, and need for some other reason to just sit still.

Let's say, for example, that you are sitting quietly in a room, not doing much of anything, just sitting there passing the time. How often do you shift your position in the chair? How many daydreams are born and flourish in the silence of the crowded empty room? Perhaps a fire engine races by as you sit there. Instead of simply hearing the sound and letting it go, isn't it more usual to comment on it? ("Why must those damn fire engines keep going past my door?") Or perhaps you enter into an entire fantasy about it:

> I wonder where the fire is? Maybe it's that empty house on the corner. What a firetrap! What do the owners expect to happen if a fire breaks out there some day?...Maybe today is that day after all. Oh lord, that's no kind of thought to be thinking, to wish the fire to happen to prove a point just because I don't approve of absentee landlords...Of course that's always been a problem in and of itself, the problem of the landlord who, because he doesn't have to live there himself, is not confronted with the physical condition of his property on a daily basis, so

he feels free to let it get run down and fall apart until a fire comes along and destroys the building…Poetic justice, that, except that the poor tenants are the ones who are left homeless and who have to put up with the miserable conditions day after day until the fire happens to bring matters to a head….

It's almost funny when you consider it: on the one hand, we just hate to do without all those entertaining ripples and waves on the surface of the pond, and on the other, we feel the deep need for some basic silence and clarity so that we can see without the distortions and confusion caused by the very same ripples and waves we created in the first place!

Somehow it's really hard to sit still and stay alert and attentive without a lot of thinking or entertainment going on.

It's not terribly difficult to concentrate on an exciting movie; it offers many crutches to support potentially weak concentration from moment to moment. If a particular moment in the movie isn't interesting, that's okay because in the very next moment something else may come along to claim attention. All you have to do is to sit back passively and let the images wash over you. Moment after moment, something always comes along to rescue you from boredom, without any real effort on your part. ("Wow! Look at that ripple!") And generally those boredom-avoiding attention-grabbers are brightly colored, loud, boisterous, and flashy, so that even the most superficial attention will yield a rich harvest of sensory stimuli and highly entertaining mental responses. In this way the pond is kept stirred up continuously, and you manage to keep yourself out of touch with your true nature.

So your first job in regulating your mind is to get your mind to sit along with your body and breath. In the beginning of Zen practice, you do this by counting your breaths.

First, seat yourself properly and allow your breathing to become regular and calm.

As you start to exhale, count that exhalation as the number one. Then, when you inhale, count that inhalation as two. Then as you exhale again, count that as three, and the following inhalation as four, and so on until you reach ten. Then start all over again on the very next breath with the number one, and repeat the counting from one through ten, over and over again. Keep doing this steadily until you can do it with full attention, not losing count, getting bored, daydreaming, or in any way interrupting your concentration. (When you reach that point in your practice, it is time to move on to a slightly different practice of counting only the exhalations or just following the breath without counting it.)

Counting the breath is a very simple thing to do, but it's not easy. One thing most people have trouble with when starting out is that they keep thinking thoughts, and find this distressing. To put this in perspective, let's take a look at the two kinds of thinking that concern us.

First of all, since the nature of the human brain is to generate thoughts continuously, nobody need feel upset when this occurs. Anyone who is not unconscious or brain-damaged will produce one thought after another. This is quite normal.

These innocent flashes of mental activity, random thoughts, are not a problem in sitting; they are simply the natural action of a healthy brain. If you tried to stop those random thoughts you would have a very hard time, and might go into a trance-like state that is not at all what zazen is about. In zazen, you are not trying to stop all thoughts from occurring.

On the other hand, there is a kind of thinking that is precisely what you must let go of when you sit, for otherwise it will dominate your mind as it has all your life. That form of thought is called discursive thought, or sequential thought; it is thought with a story line, a continuing theme, for it consists of a progression of ideas arising originally from a spontaneous and random thought and gradually turning into an elaborate theatrical or philosophical production that takes you quite effectively out of your concentration and stirs up the surface of the water of the mind.

But to deal with either random thoughts or discursive thoughts, the procedure is the same. As soon as you realize what is happening, stop, go back to one, and start counting again with renewed vigor. If you only have random thoughts from time to time, you can just keep on going and ignore them. But if the random thoughts start turning into stream-of-consciousness soliloquies, then you will find it most useful to simply return to one and start your counting again.

The principle involved is basically quite simple: nobody can really concentrate on two things at once. If this seems to be happening, in reality neither thought-object is getting your full attention. And conversely, if you really turn your attention wholly onto one focal point, there's no attention left over for such thoughts as distraction, boredom, or self-criticism.

Don't be fooled by the simplicity of this practice. It may take quite a bit of hard work until you can count from one to six, let alone ten. But there's nothing magical about the number ten! If you don't get that far but only reach two or three, that could be highly effective sitting practice too, as long as you keep returning to your counting. What is important is the consistency of attention and intention. The counting from one to ten is not an end in itself, but simply a temporary structure to help develop single-pointed attention. If "getting to ten" becomes the goal, that too can become a distraction. The numbers are only markers, not objectives. When we count, we just count. If we have to start over by the time we reach five, or even two, we just start over, without comment, without judgment. That way, you'll soon develop strong concentration, and the results will encourage you to go further. This aspect of mental training is like lifting weights. Even if you're weak when you start, regular workouts will soon produce results.

Until now, we've spoken about the three aspects of sitting—body, breath, and mind—in separate sections. But in actual practice, you'll be working on all three all the time. In fact, body, breath, and mind are inseparable. The better your posture, the more well-aligned you can make your spine, the easier your breathing will become and the quieter your mind will be. And on the other hand, the clearer your mind and the stronger your concentration, the less difficulty you will have keeping your back straight, or sitting through your discomforts without fidgeting or changing position.

With this in mind, don't be discouraged if one aspect of your practice comes along more slowly than another. Each person's practice develops differently, and usually the three aspects of sitting will mature at different rates.

In dealing with discouragement, it may be helpful to think of tuning a guitar; if the strings are tightened too much or too little, the proper pitch cannot be achieved. Similarly, in sitting, we are not trying to see how tightly we can wind the strings of our body, breath, and mind; rather, we are trying to achieve the proper pitch of stillness. We need to recognize that each moment is a fresh moment that has never existed before. Naturally experiences in our mind and body come and go. Fatigue, excitement, depression, discomfort, scattered attention, preoccupations—these are natural events, like changes in the weather. Sometimes it's hot, sometimes cold. Sometimes it's bright, sometimes cloudy. But it's always just weather. In sitting, it is just our lives, moment by moment, unfolding. Even discouragement itself is just another moment of being, not to be clung to or dreaded. Take each moment as it comes, and go on to the next unique, new moment. This is sitting.

Nonetheless, as you practice sitting sincerely and energetically, you are likely to encounter questions that are important to resolve. Here again, we see the need for a personal teacher-student relationship. Just as an athlete can be coached to regard her difficulties as guideposts to improvement, so too a sitter can be taught. But just as an athlete must train even when not under the guidance of a coach, so too the sitter must practice even in the absence of a teacher. Although a teacher is essential, also understand that sitting practice is itself a wonderful teacher. Sitting alone or in a group of peers is always valuable; it is better to practice this way than to not practice simply because you may not have easy access to a teacher.

Even so, it is worth emphasizing again that sooner or later it is *crucial* to practice with a qualified teacher you can trust and with whom you can honestly discuss your practice. No amount of reading could ever deal effectively with all the possible experiences, since these always arise intimately out of the depths of who you are. If you follow the instructions in this book carefully, though, you will have gotten a good start on basic practice, and that should sustain you until you are ready to find your teacher in person.

Part Two: Sitting

Practice is like regular exercise,
which builds strength, gracefulness, and self-confidence
to meet the situations we all face every day.
And it is like a laboratory, in which we can continuously test
our understanding to see if it is adequate or not.
If we never test our beliefs,
we cannot find out their truth or falsity.
Maezumi Roshi

PART THREE:
COMMUNITY

WHAT IS
COMMUNITY?

S O FAR, everything described could be practiced by a
solitary individual. But true Zen practice cannot be fully
experienced in all its diversity and richness by just one person alone.
Sooner or later it becomes important to join with a group of people
who together form a community of practice.

This community of practice comes out of each person's determi-
nation to achieve some fundamental understanding of what this life
really means, what this self really is.

If a buddha is one who realizes and lives enlightenment, and sitting is the deepest expression of that realization and life, then community is nothing other than going deeper and deeper into that
realization, and becoming more and more at one with that life.

This happens most readily and most fully when we are doing it
in the company of others who are doing the same thing.

There are various ways to practice with others, ranging from the
highly structured schedule and disciplines of a training center or
monastery to the less formal but equally valuable style of many

practice groups. Each form is likely to be suited to the capacities and needs of some practitioners more than others. Find the community that suits you best.The more rigorous forms offer certain advantages; the more informal groups offer others. No one form is necessarily better than another *per se*; each should be appreciated for what it offers.

Although we may not immediately see it clearly, practicing together can be very helpful in discovering that we can be naturally in harmony with all sorts of situations, with all beings and with all conditions, as well as with the many facets of our own selves. Being in harmony, though, does not necessarily imply a state of unbroken sweetness and light. Rather, harmony suggests a readiness to deal appropriately with all events and circumstances without becoming separate or alienated from either oneself or one's surroundings. Practice together is a harmony based on this single, clear realization: that everything—you, me, the whole universe as it is—is one.

Each person, each moment, and each event exists only as a result of all that has gone before it and thus is the tip of a vast iceberg of cause and effect. When we see only that tip, we miss the connections that make it one with us, and so we have the impression of conflict and separateness. But however convincing that impression may be, in sitting we can experience it more intimately. And it is in such a moment of recognition that we come face to face with the oneness that goes beyond conflict, discouragement, and the limited illusions of common sense.

Of course, that doesn't imply a passive acceptance of events or conditions. Members of the community work, both together and as individuals, to take care of everything in the best way possible. When sick, we seek proper medical care; when hungry, we feed ourselves. So it is that we take care of the eventualities and difficulties that arise in community practice.

Certainly, differences do exist, and no community is free of disagreements or friction. It's just that we try to remember that such situations are occasions for us to practice, to experience, and then to let go of our limited point of view.

A practice community—and practice itself—offers an opportunity to realize that between subject and object there is no gap, that problems tend to contain within themselves their causes and their solutions.

When we view things from this nondualistic perspective, we can see a very special, and at the same time very ordinary, harmony everywhere, always.

The Buddha is the one who realizes.
The Dharma is what is realized.
And the Sangha is the harmony of practice,
both communal and individual, in accord with the Buddha Way.
In this way, all relationships teach us,
even as we appreciate and polish each other, endlessly.
Maezumi Roshi

GROUP PRACTICE

Group practice in a Zen community like a monastery or training center usually takes some or all basic forms: daily practice, an intensive training period, and the special meditation retreat called *sesshin*.

Daily Practice

First of all, there is the day-to-day practice schedule, which differs from place to place. It usually combines several hours of daily sitting with meals, work-practice, and chanting, all according to a regular timetable. A common element in each of these activities is caretaking; taking good care of each action, each moment.

A Typical Training Day

I'll describe a typical day's schedule at the Zen center at which I trained, the Zen Center of Los Angeles. Originally modeled on a Japanese monastic curriculum, ZCLA's schedule has undergone an evolution that reflects the cultural and demographic differences of a diverse American community in which many members have jobs and family responsibilities yet wish to undertake a period of more intensive practice than they might otherwise be able to do alone. The schedule that follows, then, is offered simply as an example, not as a mandatory model. Each training center's schedule will differ to a greater or lesser degree.

A typical training day begins with dawn sitting and morning service at 5:30 A.M. At 7:00 A.M., *oryoki* breakfast is served (oryoki is a formal meal taken in the meditation hall and accompanied by liturgy), and at 8:45 A.M. communal work-practice begins. At 11:15 A.M., a 45-minute class is held, and at noon, students and teacher gather in the meditation hall for oryoki lunch followed by a rest period. From 2:00 to 4:00 P.M., caretaking work resumes, with sitting again at 4:30 P.M., followed at 5:30 P.M. by evening service and oryoki dinner.

At 7:30 P.M., evening zazen is held, and at 9:00 P.M., the schedule ends.

One of the benefits of so detailed a schedule is that it makes unnecessary the sometimes complex decisions as to how individuals should use their time, and lets the trainees develop a smooth rhythm for their day's training.

Almost all practice centers incorporate some form of communal work called *samu*. Work-practice—which is often something physical and not intellectually demanding, though in fact it can be anything at all—is more than simply work in the usual sense of getting the chores done. Rather, like every aspect of the life of Zen practice, samu is itself a form of meditation.

Washing dishes, for instance, can be sheer drudgery; we can stand at the sink impatiently trying to get it over with, resenting every minute we have to devote to such menial labor. Isn't that the way we often tackle our chores?

But there is also another way of washing dishes, in which each act is done with the same intensity of concentration and awareness we devote to zazen. Scraping off the scraps, immersing the dishes in water, rinsing them of all traces of dirt and soap, drying them and stacking them neatly in the cabinet ready for use at the next meal—this can be powerful Zen practice.

Just as a musician can become utterly absorbed in the music being played, so can we become utterly absorbed in any task we are doing. Once we give our complete attention to the task, there's nothing left over for such comments as "I hate washing dishes" or "I wish I didn't have to do this!" Our practice becomes just dishwashing— Now, this does not mean "mere, lowly dishwashing," but rather dishwashing *only*. Just as when we "just sit" there is no problem or disharmony, so when we "just wash dishes" we find it to be excellent, harmonious practice.

Of course work-practice is not limited to a Zen center or monastery. Going to school, building a house, turning a wrench, filling out a form at the office—all can be done with the same single-minded attentiveness. And even amid the busiest of lives, time can be found to practice with others.

Practicing like this in the everyday world, we come to recognize the fact of our interrelatedness with the world itself. We come to realize clearly that the community can only exist in some specific, local context, which in turn exists within a larger context, and so on. We may start very locally indeed: the cushion on which we sit, or the corner of the room in which that cushion is placed. From there, the context expands, to include the building and grounds of the meditation hall, and the neighborhood or region in which it is situated. Understanding this, we come to recognize that our own families and the families of those practicing alongside us are involved with us; they too are affected by our involvement with this practice and with each other, and they in turn are interacting and affecting us. These families have a wider circle of others—extended families, friends, co-workers, neighbors—who in turn contribute to the circumstances of their lives.

Even though we may not know many of these others, we nonetheless are affected by the simple fact of their existence. Eventually, as this realization becomes broader and more clear, we realize that we are, in fact, part of a community that includes all beings everywhere.

AN INTENSIVE TRAINING PERIOD
IN A ZEN MONASTERY

Unlike a Christian monastery in the West, a Zen monastery is not intended to be a lifelong place of seclusion in which people live a drastically different life than they would on the "outside." In some ways, the traditional Zen monastery serves more the function of a seminary or a training camp at which men and women prepare for the priesthood or train themselves for their lifelong practice in the "secular" world.

Typically, a monk or nun in Japan will spend two ninety-day training periods each year in the monastery, and in the course of a number of years may become the head of a smaller temple and leave the monastery more or less permanently. It is also not uncommon for laypersons in Japan to enter monasteries for short periods of time, ranging from a few days to a few months, to partake of a kind of training refresher course. So during the year, a Japanese monastery actually operates on a full training schedule only about half the time.

Most of the training centers that have emerged in the West follow more or less the Japanese monastic pattern. During the training period, the daily schedule of activities is expanded to place a somewhat stronger emphasis on sitting (as much as four or five hours daily in some cases); additional talks are given by the teacher; and more individual study and contact with the teacher is scheduled for the trainees. Although in Asia this kind of training is predominantly intended for monks and nuns, in the West most training-program participants are actually laypersons. Temporarily setting aside the usual routines of their lives, these training participants seem to find new awareness of their own strength and flexibility, and the perspective that emerges through training often helps them deal more creatively with families, friends, and fellow workers.

In such cases, priests and lay students may practice side by side, finding in their differences and similarities a constant challenge to make their time together one of mutual learning and growth.

Each month of the training period usually culminates in a sesshin or intensive sitting retreat, which is the third basic form of formal Zen training.

SESSHIN

The word *sesshin* comes from two Japanese words, *setsu* which means "to collect" or "to regulate," and *shin*, which means "heart" or "mind." Additionally, the word implies unifying or harmonizing one's individual practice with that of the larger group. So a sesshin is a special time devoted to collecting or regulating the heart/mind, as well as unifying or harmonizing one's own practice with that of other participants.

While sesshin is a monthly observance at many monasteries and Zen training centers, practitioners may undertake this practice only once or twice a year, as their circumstances and commitments allow.

But regardless of how often one participates in sesshin, it provides a change of pace and focus from everyday life that is a crucially important aspect of Zen training, and sesshin has a cumulative and far-reaching impact on the life of the participants. It has been said that one who has not sat sesshin has yet to fully experience Zen practice. Many people find that in sesshin the practices of sitting, working, and being alone with a diverse yet similarly attuned group of others serve to greatly heighten the sense of immediateness and personal relevance of sitting and to afford a far more visceral appreciation of Zen practice. And in the process, the individual's sense of relatedness to others—and to the teachings and the practice itself— is greatly enhanced.

Thus, for three to seven days, the trainees live, eat, sit, work, and sleep inside the monastery or Zen center.

The emphasis is on sitting, about eight to ten hours daily at most places, but there is also work-practice, chanting, talks by the teacher, and daily personal encounters between teacher and student. A rule of silence is generally observed, and all socializing, even normal eye contact, is minimized. Participants are also urged to minimize any reading or writing during that time, and of course radio, TV, and recreational reading are completely set aside. The time is to be used in the constant probing and exploration of one's own depths, and the rule of practice is to do whatever the schedule calls for in unison and silent harmony.

The day begins early, around 4:00 A.M., and ends around 9:30 P.M. Almost every moment of the day is set aside for some specific activity, with the understanding that those attending the sesshin will participate as fully in each of the scheduled activities as they possibly can.

A typical day's schedule during sesshin might go like this:

5 A.M.	wake up
5:30	zazen
	(While sitting is going on, students have private interviews with the teacher. Periods of zazen alternate with brief periods of walking meditation.)
7:05	morning liturgy
7:25	oryoki breakfast
8:45	work-practice
11:00	end of work period
11:30	zazen
12 noon	talk by the teacher/zazen
1:20 P.M.	afternoon liturgy
1:40	oryoki lunch followed by a rest period
4:00	zazen
5:25	evening liturgy
5:35	oryoki dinner or informal dinner
7:30	zazen
8:50	closing liturgy
9:00	optional zazen
10:00 P.M.	lights out

Most of the time we all lead very busy lives, with dozens of decisions and thoughts demanding our attention moment after moment. But since every activity during sesshin is scheduled, all we need do is follow the schedule wholeheartedly, and the whole issue of self-discipline, busyness, and distraction is resolved. When the schedule calls for lunch, we eat; when it says zazen, we do zazen. And because most of the activities of the day are done in a rather formal manner (that is, in a prescribed, standard way), even such minor decisions as how to take your seat or which bowl to eat from are eliminated in advance by the very form itself.

Naturally, most of us would not wish to live by a formal sesshin schedule all the time. But attending sesshin regularly during the year can bring you very close to yourself, and can build great strength and self-confidence. Moreover, sesshin can remind us just how precious our time is.

As mentioned before, the word *sesshin* literally means "to collect the mind" or "to unify the mind." This refers to the individual's experience of going deeper and deeper into his or her own noisy silence and bringing order out of chaos as the sesshin concentration deepens and the sense of integration gets stronger.

But another meaning or implication of the word *sesshin* is "to join or link minds." This aspect of sesshin is a reflection of the group practice, for even as the group is made up of individuals who have seemingly minimal contact with each other, still as the week goes on, there is created a pervasive sense of group identity and solidarity, within which personal idiosyncrasies and peculiarities are at once subordinated and expressed. It is common for us in the West to see individual and group identities as polar opposites, and we tend to feel that we must choose between them. But in sesshin, it becomes clear that both are real and compatible, and that the deepest harmony occurs when both are accorded the right appreciation and expression.

Intrinsically, sesshin is a model of life itself and requires that the community meet its own needs and recognize its own nature. There are certain arrangements that need to be made for feeding and housing the participants, there are the procedures by which the zendo is run smoothly, and there is the underlying unity of all those who practice together. There may be many individual differences of personality, style, taste, and maturity of practice; yet in sesshin, the diversity becomes harmony as the participants move through the hours of the day together, sitting, working, eating, studying, and sleeping according to the schedule, with a minimum of friction.

Experientially, it's like boiling water on the stove. By turning up the flame and not moving the kettle away from the heat, the water soon reaches boiling point. In following the schedule with all one's might, one is turning up the heat and leaving the kettle on the fire. At some precise moment, the water will boil. That is the moment of the breakthrough, when we appreciate our true nature directly. It's very interesting to see it happening; the sesshin process is the opposite of a vicious circle. As we practice together, going through all kinds of adjustments and difficulties, we slowly begin to experience our unity. As we experience it, two things happen. On the one hand, we tend to create that very state of unified mind itself, in which we are able to see oneness; simultaneously, we are strengthening and expressing this oneness as we give rise to it. And as we see each other strengthening and expressing it more and more, so it tends to be created anew. Perhaps we could call this a beneficent circle.

Sesshin leads the Zen student through confusion and scattered energies past the ego and beyond dualistic thought. It is a rugged and sobering trek, with deep valleys and high peaks. But it is in the making of the journey that the individual and the community discover and create themselves continuously from moment to moment.

Through this journey the teacher serves as a guide, having covered this ground thoroughly many times before, and aware, through personal experience, of the snares and pitfalls awaiting the beginner.

It is the teacher's responsibility to assess the needs of the individual and the group, and accordingly to regulate the pace and the rigor of the sesshin to provide the optimum level of challenge and stimulation. Through senior assistants, the teacher keeps the sesshin focused and running smoothly, and through the frequent daily encounters with each individual, the teacher gets feedback about how everyone is doing, individually and collectively.

Of course, it is also true that in a sense everyone is the teacher of everyone else. When you sit with a group you soon begin to sense a remarkable supportive energy that comes into being and that affects all those in its field. So as your sitting-neighbor helps you, you in turn also help that person.

In a fashion perhaps otherwise never normally experienced, sesshin relieves individuals of the need to break concentration even briefly. Every moment, every action can be experienced as arising from the moments and actions preceding and following it. At first, the quest for such sustained attention often seems difficult, even impossible. We are normally accustomed to doing something, then taking a break. We may be used to thinking of our usual day as consisting of hours when we are "on duty"—that is, committed to working or functioning in a certain way—and "on break," in which we are somehow free to relax and enjoy ourselves or at least to rest up and prepare for whatever demands are to come. This is a quite normal way of experiencing our time.

And yet, in sesshin, we find an opportunity to go beyond such a customary viewpoint, to explore what it really means to pay attention, moment after moment. Even during scheduled rest periods and during meals, we begin to discover in sesshin that the very texture of our moment-to-moment consciousness is far richer than we might have previously realized. We may begin to notice the subtleties of all activities: sitting or eating, pulling weeds. We discover that no two moments are alike. And as this awareness sinks in, we may begin to wonder how much of our so-called everyday lives passes unnoted, unappreciated, unused. Thus, in sesshin, we are able to discover our lives anew and, with this discovery, what it means to be alive.

Experiencing Sesshin

Most people report that their first sesshin is a most unsettling experience, at least in the beginning.

First of all, once the sesshin has formally begun, no one speaks or even makes eye-contact with anyone else. In fact, most of the normal social amenities are set aside: After the retreat formally begins, no one greets you with a cheerful "hello" each morning; no one acknowledges your presence as you pass others in the zendo or around the grounds; everyone seems to be preoccupied with the same weighty matter. All of this may prove anxiety-provoking, to the degree that any sharp departure from our familiar social setting can be a little disorienting at first. Gradually, however, once the familiar conventions are set aside, a subtle sense of relatedness in the midst of the silence begins to manifest, a deepened appreciation of shared purpose and experience quite independent of the more familiar patterns of everyday social give-and-take.

And although the strangeness will gradually wear off, that initial insecurity and degree of disorientation may give you a clue as to how far from stability and harmony the "normal" way of life actually is.

For the first three days of sesshin, the physical adjustment is also frequently quite rigorous. The muscles of the body, used to very different patterns of activity and repose, must now accommodate themselves to lengthy periods of immobility and the stress of maintaining zazen many hours more each day than they are normally used to.

But sometime between the third and fourth days, there is a point at which discomfort and fatigue peak. If, at such a juncture, you just avoid drawing any conclusions (such as "I can't stand this any more" or "I'm never going to make it" or "This isn't so tough; maybe I don't have to try so hard") and continue to practice with steady concentration, a corner will almost always be turned. There is a curious and most welcome "second wind" that comes about on the third or fourth day, and from that point onward, time often seems to accelerate to the end of sesshin. By the third or fourth day, too, the body has greatly adjusted to the physical stresses, and the discomfort or pain have become more familiar and less overwhelming, so that there is a real feeling of having gotten over the hump.

At this point, sesshin may become very closely integrated into oneself, so that there is no separation between the demands of the sesshin schedule and one's own personal needs and rhythms.

To have sesshin
means to have the chance to really concentrate,
to realize who we really are.
Maezumi Roshi

REALIZING THE HARMONY

Perhaps this process of reaching a crisis and then passing through it into calm waters is characteristic not only of sitting sesshin, but of all the other aspects of life as well.

If you pursue this practice even for a little while, there generally comes a day when you walk into that silent room with all the zafus neatly lined up and the faint smell of incense in the air and you feel welcome and at home.

As the others come in and take their seats, there is no longer a nagging sense of isolation and noncommunication. In this silence you sense the real communication expressing itself with each inhalation and exhalation.

What has happened?

One thing may be that you are beginning to experience the harmony of community, knowing that it doesn't depend on conversation or on bridging gaps. There is no need either to gloss over differences or to create polite distractions. As we sit together, each of us uniquely ourself, we can also appreciate our common humanity, our membership in a community that is vastly bigger and more inclusive than our differences.

In a way, it's even misleading to speak of sitting alone or together. No matter how many people are sitting in the room, there is still only that great reality with each sitter at its exact center. In that sense, since each one is the whole universe, each one is always alone. The "whole universe" is always alone, literally "all one," since it includes everything and everyone throughout space and time. There is nothing outside of it to keep it—to keep *you*—company.

But at the same time, and by the same token, nobody ever sits alone, since each of us contains the infinite diversity and variety of all reality.

It is the realization that these two seemingly opposite perspectives are mutually compatible—are, in fact, the very same thing—that allows us to enter into the spirit of community together. You may not realize this in one sitting, or even in one sesshin, but if you practice consistently it will certainly become clear. Simply going forward, step by step, at your own pace will get you there, just as walking gently through a mist can, in time, get you just as wet as would standing in the pouring rain.

So, in your practice set aside any impatience with "results." And in so doing, you can give rise, naturally and over time, to the development of an appreciation of what this practice of being still, what this life—your life—really is.

*This undivided life of the buddhas and ancestors
is manifesting as difference, as diversity.
Please focus on how to appreciate this
undivided and diverse life meaningfully
and how to contribute in some way
to decreasing the pain around us.*
Maezumi Roshi

AFTERWORD

A T THE END of a book, it is tempting to tie everything up neatly with a conclusion. This book, however, has no conclusion; it is a book of beginnings.

What we find in the day-to-day practice of Zen is somehow ordinary and extraordinary at the same time.

In the midst of the usual, we learn to pause, to allow our innate intelligence and wisdom to function, to make a difference in how we appreciate the great complex dance of cause and effect, and to enter into that dance more and more fully and caringly. We become better able to appreciate forms and the formless, the relative and absolute, being still and still moving.

You are already writing the remainder of the book, which, although invisible, is endless.

A final word of encouragement: whatever happens in your life and practice, just take note of it and keep going on that long and gentle walk.

Remember who you are, and keep on going.

And forget about that, and keep on going.

FREQUENTLY
ASKED QUESTIONS

Should I try to make my mind blank?

A blank mind is not what sitting is about. To sit is to be at home, to be upright; it is to be intimate, relaxed, and yet alert. Without daydreaming, thinking, or blanking out, we count or watch our breath and allow experiences to pass unpursued and unavoided. Gradually, in sitting, a deeper and clearer awareness of who we are, of what our life is, becomes possible. The illusory gap between inner and outer worlds is (gradually or suddenly) seen for what it is, and in this way, we can be more fully in touch with our world and relate to it more compassionately and productively.

What do I do with my feelings/emotions?

When sitting, it's not at all unusual to become more aware of feelings and emotions that are normally just below the surface of your awareness, since when you sit, you tend to quiet down enough to notice more of your internal goings-on. This quieting down may initially allow those feelings to emerge, just as darkness allows the stars to "come out" at night. When this happens, just be aware of the experience, letting it come and go. Remember that feelings are neither good nor bad in themselves, but are just what's going on with you at a given moment. What matters is how you relate to what's going on. In general, if the experience is pleasant, don't try to prolong it, and if it's unpleasant, don't try to avoid or squelch it. Just notice it. Then, gently continue sitting. This approach will be generally helpful in dealing with all the normal ups and downs of everyday life.

Sometimes I don't feel calm and peaceful when I sit. Am I doing something wrong?

Not at all. If the wind blows and the trees sway back and forth, is the sky doing something wrong? How we feel simply shows us what's going on. Letting such experiences come and go without trying to rigidly control or censor them, or covering them up to look prettier may not be so easy, but it is a direct and personal way to encounter them. In this unvarnished acceptance of our changing states of mind, we can begin to see that transient thoughts and feelings are just that: transient. Feelings and thoughts do not define who we are; they are just part of the weather of our inner world. At any given point, your sitting may or may not be calm and peaceful; just be with yourself as you are, even if it's not how you might wish you would be. Of course, some feelings go beyond weather, which changes from day to day, hour to hour. These feelings may be part of a longer-term pattern, and may require special attention.

Sometimes I'm so emotionally upset I can't sit, and I wonder if the sitting is doing more harm than good.

If this continues over a prolonged period of time (several weeks or more), it may be that you would be wise to consult with a psychotherapist. Contrary to what some believe, psychotherapy (and even psychopharmacology) and sitting are not mutually exclusive or rival practices; they should actually complement each other. Just as we need to care for physical ailments, so too emotional stresses deserve careful and loving attention. Above all, sitting is not an ascetic practice to test the limits of one's tolerance for psychic or physical

95

pain. If you feel consistent emotional upset, check in with your teacher, if you have one, and look for a therapist who understands and can work with the relationship between spiritual practice and emotional development. To make use of psychotherapy is not an indication of spiritual failure or some lapse in practice, but rather a matter of wisely and compassionately taking care of one's real needs on whatever levels they exist.

Isn't sitting just for my own well-being essentially selfish?

When you do something that nourishes and centers you and enables you to be more compassionate and loving to the others in your life, it isn't selfish. To really awaken to the meaning of your life is to study yourself and take yourself far beyond narrow ideas of "self" and "other." Seeing this, if you still feel selfish sitting, you may begin to learn something about how you see yourself in relationships. And, learning this, you may find your views changing. Sit with the feelings deeply, and allow them to come and go

I find it difficult to sit because I am such an active person.

Activity is not always a hindrance; in sitting, really practice actively being with yourself without getting lost in busyness, and become more stable in your activity. A pyramid is very stable, sitting massively on the earth; a gyroscope is very active, spinning rapidly, yet at the same time very stable. If you can't sit like a pyramid, sit like a gyroscope.

Is breath-counting the main form of Zen meditation?

Breath counting is the usual introductory practice, which enables you to go on to subsequent forms and eventually set aside forms as such, and just sit. But even very experienced meditators continue to use the breath as an anchor in sitting by simply following the breath or being the breath itself.

How long do I need to practice counting my breaths?

Counting the breaths is a practice that initially builds your capacity for sustained concentration. It helps you focus your mind and enables you to see clearly whether you're really concentrating or whether your mind is wandering. Keeping the numbers sharp and clear, you can tell you're on the right track. Losing count or forgetting where you are immediately shows you your attention has wandered. Whenever thoughts arise or your attention wanders, the thing to do is just go back to "one" and begin again, without comment and without judgment. You also might think of breath counting as an exercise for the mind: it builds strength, balance, and stamina. When you've developed these capacities a bit, there are other, more demanding forms, such as koan study or *shikantaza*, to practice. But even after years of practice, it can be most helpful to use breath counting as a kind of warmup for the first few minutes each time you sit. In fact, truly sitting with your breath can be a lifelong meditation practice in itself.

What can I do throughout my day that will help my sitting? How does sitting transfer into my everyday activities?

Sitting and everyday activities are not necessarily two different things. Sitting involves two basics: stillness of body and mind, and clarity of attention. Whatever you do during the day, you can use that activity as a kind of meditation practice by doing it *thoroughly*. That is, if you are sitting, just sit; driving, just drive; cooking, just cook—the single-minded involvement in each activity helps develop the capacity for paying attention. By practicing in this way, you naturally calm down and become more aware. The more you do this, the more your daily activities will benefit and the deeper your sitting will become.

I notice a lot of past events keep popping into my mind. What does this mean?

Normally this is part of a kind of psychic digesting process in which we process events from the past that we may need to assimilate more fully. This is a natural process and need not be of concern in itself. However, if this happens continually (as opposed to just occasionally), or if the memories or feelings are very distressing, it may be an indication of events that you need to attend to. Take good care of yourself, and if this can be facilitated by seeking professional help, do so. Again, the basic rule of thumb about anything that tends to recur in your practice is to neither ignore it nor pursue it while you are sitting—but this principle should not be taken to mean that things that arise don't need to be acknowledged and eventually dealt with!

The same thoughts keep recurring. What does this mean?

Thoughts often recur as a result of certain recurrent or similar causes. When these causes change, the thoughts will change also. Meanwhile, the practice of sitting can gradually affect the ways in which we experience these recurring thoughts, allowing us to be less habituated, less caught up in them, and able to see them from a more compassionate and skillful perspective. If these thoughts are particularly disturbing, it is crucial that you check in with a teacher or therapist. If they are not, then just let them go.

I get sleepy during zazen. How can I stay awake?

First of all, make sure that you are getting sufficient sleep at night. If you are and still find sleepiness a problem during your sitting, it may be helpful to occasionally focus your attention at your hairline for a few breaths, then return to natural regular breathing. Opening your eyes wider for a time may also help. But sometimes, sleepiness just happens, and it's important not to get caught up in judgment or self-recrimination. However, if the sleepiness persists for a long time, it may be a sign that some emotional concerns need addressing more directly, and that the sleepiness is an unconscious attempt to keep them at bay. Here again is where you may find consulting with a qualified teacher or counselor especially useful.

It's difficult for me to keep my eyes open. Can I close them?

Most folks find that closing the eyes tends to lead to either drowsiness or daydreaming, and so keeping the eyes slightly open helps them avoid this. Others, however, may find that the struggle to keep their eyes open is in itself a greater distraction. If you can keep your eyes slightly open while sitting, that's best. If not, and you can stay alert and focussed with them closed, then that's okay too. Or, if you're very drowsy, try opening your eyes very wide. Do what works best for you.

It's difficult for me to make time to sit daily. Any suggestions?

We may find it difficult to make time to exercise regularly, brush our teeth, or pay the bills. But when we really appreciate the need to do something, we make time for it. The "difficulty" we have making time for these things is a clue as to what importance we attach to them, what priority we give them. If you prioritize sitting highly enough, you'll find you have time to do it. If you get up twenty minutes earlier in the morning, you will have given yourself an extra twenty minutes to sit.

How do I stop my mind from jumping thought to thought?

Have you ever seen a young puppy being trained to "stay"? The trainer will gently but persistently repeat the command and perhaps press the puppy's hindquarters into a sitting position. A skillful trainer will not become angry or frustrated with the puppy, but will patiently and gently continue to train it. This is not a bad model for training the mind. The key ingredients are persistence, consistency, and gentleness.

How can something so simple as counting my breath be so difficult?

Probably precisely because it *is* so simple. But simple is not the same as easy. And because we are so used to entertaining content in our thoughts, the simplicity of breath counting may at first be quite daunting. Once we are past the novelty of this practice, we may feel that it is quite repetitious, even boring—"Ho hum, been here, done this." Such a feeling is the result of not yet really paying attention completely. So the best thing to do when having such difficulties is to take them as a sign that one needs to pay closer attention to *each moment of each breath*. Doing this, you'll develop a greater capacity to focus your mind, and you'll find that your experience of the difficulty dissipates.

How is "zazen" different from "meditation"?

Meditation is a very general term describing many disciplines, of which zazen or sitting is the one this book describes. Similarly, running is a specific type of physical exercise.

I thought this practice was supposed to bring me peace, but I feel agitated. Why?

In sitting, you are setting aside usual work and play routines. Doing so, you may become aware of thoughts and feelings that normally haven't registered consciously. Such agitation may simply be a natural reaction to the temporary suspension of your more familiar environmental supports (such as busyness, movement, sensory stimuli). In this case, the agitation generally subsides before very long. If it persists, it may be due to other causes, and may need to be addressed more directly through additional means.

I can't get my mind to quiet down. Should I just give up?

Not at all! If your mind is noisy, sit with it, hang out with your unquiet mind, make friends with it. Your job isn't to beat it into submission, but to bring body and mind together in a respectful and compassionate way. Perhaps the problem is a wish to control your mind before you've even gotten to know it. Try to relax into the unquiet and bear witness to it rather than fighting to change it.

Can I get "addicted" to sitting?

In a way, zazen is the opposite of addiction: it is the way of freedom from clinging, the freedom to experience each moment unvarnished and complete in itself. But if you try to use sitting to numb out, create blissful states, or avoid yourself, then that can become a problematic kind of addiction. Numbness or even bliss is not what sitting is about. But sitting can also become a "positive addiction," like regular exercise or any other good habit. When you deeply realize that your sitting is not just a technique for altering your consciousness, that it actually is you living your life in its most essential and intimate immediacy, then the addiction question no longer applies.

When is the best time of day to sit?

Whenever you are most consistently able to do so. This may be first thing in the morning for many, while others find the evening best, or even midday. The important thing is not what the clock says, but your own steady practice. It's a good idea, though, to pick a time and stay with it, rather than waiting for the perfect opportunity to open up and invite you in—because it never will!

Is there a problem with meditating right after eating?

It's better to sit when your stomach is not full; a full stomach can interfere with breathing and may also create a tendency toward drowsiness.

Sitting seems like a good time for problem-solving.

Make sure you use your sitting time for sitting, not for other activities. When problem-solving, do that. When sitting, just sit. And if you find yourself so focused on problem-solving, don't beat yourself up about it; just take care of business and then sit. Or sit and then take care of business.

Why do some people burn incense during zazen?

Some people find that the familiar smell of a light incense (not too strong or perfumey) can be conducive to creating a helpful ambience. It's certainly not necessary—but perhaps you might find it valuable.

Sometimes when I am sitting, I feel like I am floating up and down. Is that normal?

Such experiences are not uncommon when we begin to sit. They are not particularly significant, and are neither "supposed to happen" nor "not supposed to happen." They only become significant if you let them interfere with your practice. Otherwise, they're like clouds in the sky. After you've been sitting awhile, they'll tend to fade away. Again, the basic rule about all experiences during sitting is: if you like it, don't run after it, and if you don't like it, don't run away from it.

I like to meditate while I'm running. Is that okay?

Many runners find running similar to meditative states. That's fine—as long as you watch where you're going and don't hurt yourself. But you should also be aware that in running you generate certain chemicals called endorphins, which stimulate the pleasure centers of the brain, giving rise to the "runner's high," a kind of blissful state. This pleasant state should not be confused with sitting practice. When you run, just run; when you sit, just sit.

Can I shift around during sitting if my legs hurt?

If you're uncomfortable, try letting the discomfort be, without immediately moving away from it. If it becomes too painful, of course, you may simply have to adjust your posture. If you are careful to establish the proper posture when you first take your seat, you are unlikely to have to move much, if at all. And finally, know your capabilities realistically and work gently to increase them. Stretching exercises like those in Appendix I may greatly enhance your flexibility and thus your comfort in zazen.

My feet fall asleep when I sit, and when I stand up I fall down. Is this normal?

Feet and legs falling asleep is quite normal. Just don't be in too big a hurry to stand up after sitting, and massage the soles of your feet with your knuckles to restore circulation before you stand. And if you have some physical condition that makes it inadvisable to sit on a zafu or a bench, use a chair. But be assured: no one has ever suffered lasting damage because their legs fell asleep during zazen!

Is zazen a religion?

No, zazen is a practice that may be done within the context of any religious tradition or without any religious reference at all. There are, for example, Roman Catholic priests and nuns, as well as Jews and rabbis, who practice or even teach zazen. There are also atheists, agnostics, and many secular practitioners doing so. Zazen is not predicated upon any belief system, but is both an expression of and a way of deepening one's own appreciation of life.

What's the story with bowing?

At some practice centers, people do prostrations or bows before or after sitting or liturgy. Bowing is a way we use the whole body to express deep respect and appreciation for our teachers, ourselves, our fellow beings, and all reality. It is also a way of unifying our body and mind and of putting in perspective our relationship to all that exists, from the greatest to the most minute. To the degree that bowing is unfamiliar, it may initially seem artificial or exotic, perhaps even giving rise to some sense of resentment or resistance. That's understandable. But if such feelings persist, perhaps we are seeing the degree to which we cling to a narrow worldview. Basically, however, bowing can be a quite wonderful portal to our development as practitioners and as people. But ultimately, just as with sitting and any other activity: When bowing, just bow.

Some centers have chanting and ritual. Why?

If you are curious about bowing or chanting, you may find it interesting to try doing it, just for the experience. And if you find that either practice bothers you, it may be even more interesting to be with your opinions and emotional responses to such practices. Ultimately, of course, if you don't want to bow or chant, that's up to you. Don't let it get in the way of sitting.

I just want to learn to relax. Will sitting help?

At the most basic levels of Zen practice, sitting and breathing quietly while quieting the mind can be deeply relaxing, as well as enhancing clarity of thought and the ability to concentrate. There is much more to sitting than this, but if this is your interest, then by all means sit.

Should I concentrate on a certain part of my body?

Not necessarily. When you sit, your focus of attention is on your breath. When you are in a sitting posture, your breathing will naturally slow and deepen and tend to move from the lungs to the abdomen. In this way, you may experience your abdominal muscles as the prime movers of the air into and out of your body. When you are working with a teacher, you may receive more specific guidance regarding the placement of your attention, such as belly breathing or focusing on the palm of your left hand, but to start, let your focus be on breathing rather than on body parts. This way you are less likely to have difficulties with muscle tension that may inadvertently arise if you attempt more advanced techniques prematurely.

Should my breath be deep? Slow?

By carefully arranging the body in the proper posture, you will find that your breath becomes deeper and slower quite naturally, without special effort on your part. Don't rush yourself. It'll happen. But however your breathing is, just practice with that.

I can't always sit everyday or for very long. Is that okay?

To sincerely do the best you can is always okay. Don't let your sitting practice become a source of guilt or shame. If you want to be compassionate toward others, you must be compassionate with yourself. Even a few minutes a few times a week is a good start.

If my thoughts get very upsetting during a period of sitting, should I stop?

As with physical pain, psychic distress is a personal thing. The key word in this question is "very." Don't traumatize yourself just to prove that you can take it. But also, don't necessarily avoid the first sign of distress. Let yourself sit with your experience without resisting it. Should it start to become too much to bear, take a break. If it persists the next time you sit, don't ignore it. Pain of any sort may be a warning of some condition that needs skilled care. If you are in psychotherapy or feel that you may need to be, recurring upsetting thoughts may indicate an area of your life to examine with your therapist.

I have very young children. Is there any way to include children in this practice?

Many parents of infants or toddlers take turns babysitting so that each gets a chance to sit. Some parents find that their children like to hang out with them while they are sitting. Once the novelty wears off, most children will accept sitting as a part of household life and may even want to do it (or some version of it) with the grownups. The most important thing to communicate to your kids is that they aren't being deprived of loving attention and that your silence and immobility is not a rejection of them.

APPENDICES

APPENDIX I
EXERCISES
TO HELP YOU SIT

Some stretching movements can help to open the body and to develop comfortable and stable zazen posture. These positions help us work with our physical blocks and tensions. Although each position has an ideal form, in which the spine and tendons are fully extended, the joints and breathing channels opened and relaxed, don't worry if you can't quite get your body completely into the ideal pose.

Experience each stretch as fully as you can and just relax into the most complete extension you can comfortably hold. Any straining or forced effort develops new physical tensions and reinforces existing stress. Anything more than mild discomfort is a warning. Please heed it! It may take longer to finish your stretches that way, but you won't injure yourself. Work gently at the edges of your limits. Slow, steady practice has tremendous power.

You'll find that if you practice the following exercises regularly, the bodily pain you experience during sitting will diminish significantly over time.

BUTTERFLY

(See the figures below.) Sit up straight on the ground. Put the soles of the feet together, hold the toes with your hands and bring the heels into the groin as close as comfortably possible. Work the knees up and down. This loosens the legs and hips. Then, keeping the back straight, lean over the feet. In holding this and other postures, do not tense the muscles. Inhale deeply and exhale an "ahhhh" sound. This helps release tension in the tendons and joints.

NECK ROTATIONS

(Not shown.) Slowly rotate the head counterclockwise as far as you can. Then rotate clockwise. Repeat several times.

HEAD-TO-KNEE

(See the figure below.) Sit up straight on the ground, legs stretched out and together. Keeping the arms straight and the back of the legs flat on the ground, reach for the toes. Lean down slowly with the lower back still straight. When you are as far down as is comfortable, hold the toes for support. If you can't reach the toes, simply grasp the ankles or the legs comfortably. Again, relax the muscles and breathe from the lower abdomen while holding this position.

ARM SWING

(Not shown.) Standing comfortably with the feet parallel to each other, let the hands hang in front of the hips, palms facing each other. Keep the arms slightly in front of the body and swing the arms out to the side. Swing the right arm out to the right and the left arm out to the left. The upswing should reach just above the head, and in the downswing, the wrists should cross in front of the pelvis. Let the momentum of the turn move the arms. Repeat several times.

LEG SPREAD

(See the figure below.) Sit up straight on the ground, legs stretched out in front. Stretch the legs apart as wide as is comfortable. Keeping the back straight and bracing yourself with your hands, lean forward and down as far as is comfortable. Breathe into the lower abdomen. Come back up. Keeping the spine straight, lean the left side over the left leg, hold, and concentrate on breathing. Come back up. Keeping the spine straight, lean the left side over toward the right leg; hold, and concentrate on breathing.

TRUNK TWIST

(See the figure on the following page.) Stand with the left foot forward and the right foot about three feet back and turned to the side at a 70-degree angle. Facing left, stretch the arms out to the sides horizontally, palms down. Gently turn from side to side feeling the turn through the shoulders, the back, the hips, and the legs. Then reverse this, putting the right foot forward and the left foot about three feet back and turned to the side. Facing right, stretch the arms out horizontally to the sides, palms down. Gently turn from side to side, feeling the turn through the whole body.

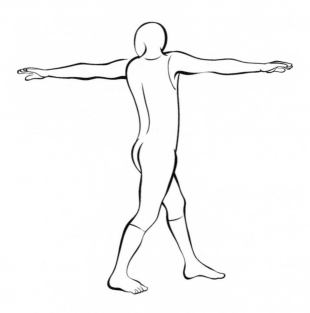

LEG STRETCH 1

(See the figure below.) Sit in the Burmese, half-lotus, or full-lotus position. Gently lower your torso in the direction of one knee until it begins to get uncomfortable. Don't strain to reach it. Hold for a count of ten, straighten up, relax, and repeat. Repeat the exercise for one minute with each knee.

NECK TWIST

(Not shown.) Sitting comfortably, keep the head upright and turn the head to the left, then to the right, several times. Then turn the head to the left and hold, feeling the breathing in the front of the chest. Turn to the right and hold, feeling the breathing in the front of the chest.

LEG STRETCH II

(See the figure below.) Sit with the left leg stretched out in front of you. Fold the right leg so the top of the foot is on the thigh of the outstretched leg. Gently press the right knee toward the ground for a count of ten. Then switch legs.

NECK HANGS

(Not shown.) Sit in a comfortable position with the back straight and relaxed. Hang the head forward and concentrate on breathing into the back of the neck and between the shoulder blades. Hang the head to the left with the ear directly over the left shoulder, while concentrating on breathing into the right side of the neck and the right shoulder. Hang the head to the right with the ear directly over the right shoulder, while concentrating on breathing into the left side of the neck and the left shoulder. Let the head hang back while concentrating on breathing into the thorax.

ABDOMINAL BREATHING

(Not shown.) Lie flat on your back on the floor. Make sure your abdomen isn't constricted by a belt or tight clothing. Then take a heavy book or similarly weighted object—any 3–5-pound weight will do—and place it on your abdomen below the navel. Now watch the weight rise as you inhale, and fall as you exhale. Notice how far the weight moves up and down.

Now, using only the belly muscles, see if you can make the weight rise higher on the inhalation, and sink deeper on the exhalation. Take your time and don't rush. Feel which muscles are involved. Do this for two or three minutes.

Then immediately get into your sitting position, and as you breathe, notice that the same abdominal muscles are used as in the exercise. After doing this for a few days just before you sit, you should develop a clearer "feel" for the lower abdominal wall.

APPENDIX II:
WEB RESOURCES

The following online resources may be helpful in locating a qualified teacher or community to sit with:

Buddhanet
www.buddhanet.net/worlddir.htm

International Research Institute for Zen Buddhism
www.iijnet.or.jp/iriz/zen_centers/country_list_e.html

Manjushri Communications
www.manjushri.com/TEMPLES/temple.html

Open Directory Project
www.dmoz.org/Society/Religion_and_Spirituality/Buddhism/
Centers_and_Groups_by_Region

The Zen Center of Los Angeles
www.zencenter.org

APPENDIX III
FURTHER READING

Appreciate Your Life

Taizan Maezumi

Taizan Maezumi Roshi, founder of the Zen Center of Los Angeles, has been little known in print despite his far-reaching impact on the practice of Zen in the West. This first collection of Maezumi Roshi's talks vividly conveys the compassion, humor, and penetrating wisdom of this seminal Zen teacher encouraging and challenging his American students.

Bearing Witness

Bernie Glassman

The co-founder of the Peacemaker Community tells of his personal odyssey from the White House steps to Auschwitz to the Bowery, into the heart of all suffering and joy. Perhaps the most human recent account of the unfolding of compassion in everyday life.

Cutting Through Spiritual Materialism *and* Shambhala: The Sacred Path of the Warrior
Chogyam Trungpa

Since his journey from Tibet and Europe to the United States, the author of these two modern classics has emerged as one of the most influential Buddhist teachers in the West. In a unique voice, Trungpa Rinpoche conducts a penetrating examination of what the practitioner encounters along the way. These two volumes go well beyond the categories of "Tibetan" or even "Buddhist" teachings. A wellspring of wisdom for all who cultivate the life of the spirit.

Instructions to the Cook
Bernie Glassman

In this radical and quintessentially contemporary re-presenting of teachings from the thirteenth-century Zen master Eihei Dogen's classic of the same name, the Brooklyn-born American Jewish Zen teacher presents a vivid and profound reminder that the teachings are alive, timeless, and go beyond all cultural bounds.

The Mind of Clover
Robert Aitken

Extending the principles of Buddhist ethics and morality from the life of the individual to the relationship of the individual to the community and the planet, the beloved elder brother of first-generation American Zen teachers addresses the values of a modern world from an ancient wellspring.

Zen Mind, Beginner's Mind

Shunryu Suzuki

In this gentle gem we are invited into the heart of a major modern master, founder of the San Francisco Zen Center, whose teachings embody an awakened perspective, transcending culture and place.

ABOUT THE AUTHOR

JOHN DAISHIN BUKSBAZEN is a Zen Buddhist priest at the Zen Center of Los Angeles.

Ordained in 1968, he trained for more than a decade with Taizan Maezumi Roshi while serving as publishing editor of the Zen writings series produced by ZCLA and also as a pastoral counselor.

A psychotherapist and psychoanalyst in private practice in Santa Monica, California, he is on the faculty of the Advanced Psychotherapy Training Program at the Southern California Psychoanalytic Institute, where he did his psychoanalytic training.

ABOUT WISDOM

Wisdom Publications, a not-for-profit publisher, is dedicated to preserving and transmitting important works from all the major Buddhist traditions as well as related East-West themes.

To learn more about Wisdom, or to browse our books on-line, visit our website at wisdompubs.org.

If you would like to receive our mail-order catalog, please write to:

Wisdom Publications
199 Elm Street
Somerville, Massachusetts 02144 USA
Telephone: (617) 776-7416 • Fax: (617) 776-7841
Email: sales@wisdompubs.org • www.wisdompubs.org

THE WISDOM TRUST

As a not-for-profit publisher, Wisdom Publications is dedicated to the publication of fine Dharma books for the benefit of all and dependent upon the kindness and generosity of sponsors in order to do so. If you would like to make a donation to Wisdom, please do so through our Somerville office. If you would like to help sponsor the publication of a book, please write or email us for more information.

Thank you.

Wisdom Publications is a nonprofit, charitable 501(c)(3) organization affiliated with the Foundation for the Preservation of the Mahayana Tradition (FPMT).

NOVICE TO MASTER
An Ongoing Lesson in the Extent of My Own Stupidity
Soko Morinaga Roshi
Translated by Belenda Attaway Yamakawa
0-86171-319-2, cloth, $19.95

Funny and urgent, vivid and economic, *Novice to Master* reads like a great novel and yet is a true-to-life spiritual autobiography. In detailing his days as a Buddhist monk, the author employs an almost ferocious honesty that plants us squarely into his world.

"A moving story of somebody, much like you or me, who discovers for himself the timeless value of Zen. Morinaga's direct wisdom bubbles through the pages."—Tom Chetwynd, author, *Zen and the Kingdom of Heaven*

ON ZEN PRACTICE
Body, Breath, and Mind
Edited by Taizan Maezumi Roshi and Bernie Glassman
Foreword by Robert Aitken
0-86171-315-x, paper, $16.95

This updated landmark volume makes available for the first time in decades the teachings that were formative to a whole generation of American Zen teachers and students. Conceived as the essential Zen primer, *On Zen Practice* addresses every aspect of practice: beginning practice, chanting, sesshin, shikantaza, working with Mu, the nature of koans, and more.

On Zen Practice's contributors are regarded as some of modern Zen's foremost teachers, and are largely responsible for Zen's steady growth in America. This newly refined volume is an unmatched teaching and reference tool for today's Zen practitioner.

FOR MORE ZEN AND BUDDHIST BOOKS, VISIT WISDOMPUBS.ORG